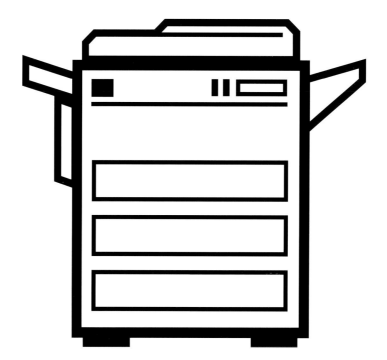

IF YOU'RE INTERESTED IN USING ICONS FROM THE BOOK, PLEASE CONTACT MUTABOR IN HAMBURG

IMPRINT
LINGUA UNIVERSALIS
- ->

MUTABOR Design, Hamburg
www.mutabor.com

Written by: Johannes Plass
Design: Beatrice de Joncheere, Anna Linder, Carsten Raffel
Translation/Editorial Agency: Dieter Schlichting, Dr. Anke Paravicini

Edited by R. Klanten
Published by Die Gestalten Verlag, Berlin · London

Bibliographic information published by Die Deutsche Bibliothek
Die Deutsche Bibliothek lists this publication in the Deutsche Nationalbibliografie; detailed bibliographic data is available in the Internet at
http://dnb.ddb.de.

© dgv- Die Gestalten Verlag GmbH & Co.KG, Berlin 2004
ISBN 3-89955-033-1

For your local dgv distributor please check www.die-gestalten.de
Respect copyright, encourage creativity.

This book belongs to:

MUTABOR LINGUA UNIVERSALIS
Global **Wordless** Understanding – Die Gestalten Verlag

Chief Creative Icon Designers:

Axel Domke, Steffen Mackert, Jens Uwe Meyer, Heinrich Paravicini, Johannes Plass, Carsten Raffel

Senior Creative Icon Designers:

Anna Bertermann, Daniel Bognar, Julia Bünger, Simone Campe, Michael Daiminger, Kristina Düllmann, Christian Dvorak, Silke Eggers, Jens Grothe, Mareile Hanke, Tanja Heinemann, Monika Hoinkis, Jessica Hoppe, Beatrice de Joncheere, Thomas Kappes, Anna Linder, Annika Marquardsen, Paul Neulinger, Catherine Nippe, Sven Ritterhoff, Trixi Rossi, Steffi Tomasek, Behruz Tschaitschan, Astrid Varrasquinho, Bernhard Uhlig, Michelle Wirtz

Administration and Organization: Barbara Stolley-Rögels

SPECIAL THANKS
LINGUA UNIVERSALIS, DEDICATION
- ->

We dedicate this book to the German painter, graphic designer and commercial artist Karl Schulpig (1884–1948), the first picture logo and pictogram designer of the modern age we know of.

His work for German companies in the 1920s and 1930s remained undiscovered for a long time. It was the Californian design scene of the 1980s, which looked to German design of the 1920s and 1930s, that once again quoted and distributed the reduced pictorial style of Karl Schulpig. In the 1990s the symbols made their way back to their German home via their documentation in the widespread »New Logo« books by Gerry Rosentswieg. The impact the picture symbols had in Germany over the last ten years is well known and has often been described.

So, together with the Old Master, let's enjoy the return of the picture symbol and let's send his philosophy on another journey with this book.

| **KARL SCHULPIG** |
- - - - - - - - - - - - - - - - - - - -
KRAFT-VERSICHERUNG, ALLIANZ

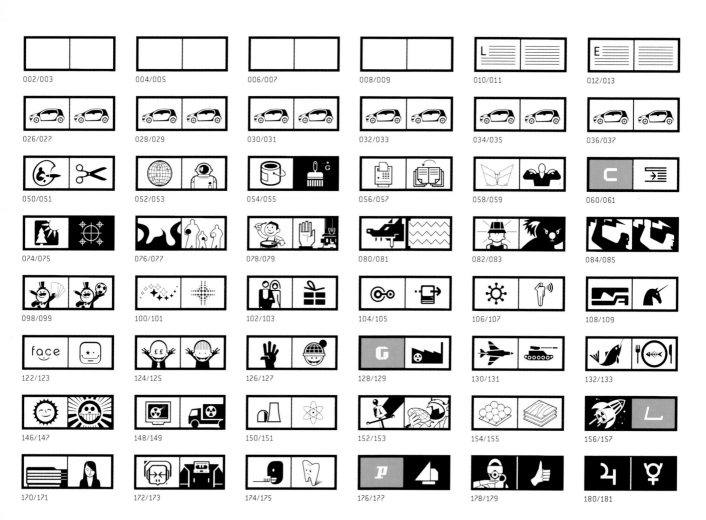

002/003   004/005   006/007   008/009   010/011   012/013

026/027   028/029   030/031   032/033   034/035   036/037

050/051   052/053   054/055   056/057   058/059   060/061

074/075   076/077   078/079   080/081   082/083   084/085

098/099   100/101   102/103   104/105   106/107   108/109

122/123   124/125   126/127   128/129   130/131   132/133

146/147   148/149   150/151   152/153   154/155   156/157

170/171   172/173   174/175   176/177   178/179   180/181

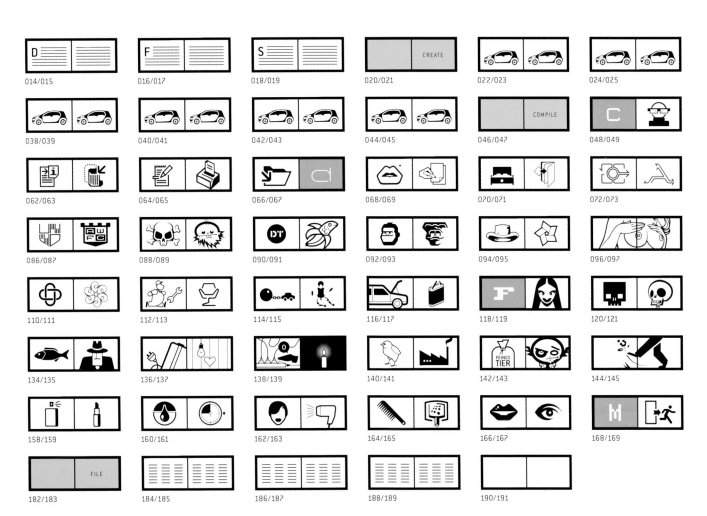

014/015 016/017 018/019 020/021 022/023 024/025

038/039 040/041 042/043 044/045 046/047 048/049

062/063 064/065 066/067 068/069 070/071 072/073

086/087 088/089 090/091 092/093 094/095 096/097

110/111 112/113 114/115 116/117 118/119 120/121

134/135 136/137 138/139 140/141 142/143 144/145

158/159 160/161 162/163 164/165 166/167 168/169

182/183 184/185 186/187 188/189 190/191

Mille dierum post publicationem libri nostri primi praeterito offerimus nunc librum secundum sub titulo »Lingua Universalis« symbolis recentibus mille et trecentibus continentem. Sic diem ex die spatii illius temporis 1,3 symbola fere imaginum in domo nostra prolata sunt quae hoc in opere nunc praesentabimus convenienter.

Primum librum quidem »Lingua Grafica« notas imagium mille trecentas et unam praesentantem ad tempus sufficere putares. Immo vero: adventus operis huius prosperrimus undam vastam novorum signorum procreavit.

Amatoribus vel amicis spectatoribusque libri nostri gratias maximas habemus eisque imprimis qui ex opere sive labore nostro invitationem ad collaborationem domo nostra intellegebant. Imitatoribus vero non legitimis eatenus grati esse volumus ut nihilominus genus distinctum nostrae designationis disseminari adiuvent.

Hic praesentamus subtiliorem et rerum novarum pleniorem collectionem quasi completam. Magis magisque notae imaginum in usu sunt in regionibus adhuc ad verba pertinentibus. Ubicumque argumenta in linguis diversis perceptanda, ubi complexio argumentorum imagine melius celeriterque quam lingua perspicienda sunt, signa ista picta exoriri solent.

Adhuc usus notarum imaginum cadebat in rationem tum securitatis tum monitus cognitionisque, non modo quod attinet locos veros sed etiam regionem tabularum ad computationem utilium. Sed hodie notae nobis prosunt plus etiam ad descriptionem et definitionem mercium per se vel ad instigationem emacitatis. Mercatu novo novas species graphicas petente significationes signorum mutantur et variantur subiectae normis graphicis unitatis corporativae.

Signorum conformatio idest signorum forma et genus indicant et eorum originem et auctorem aut eorum destinationem communicationis. »Lingua Universalis« indicabit utrumque partem: partim signa modo nostro formata partim ad alteram destinationem accomodata erint.

Iterum aperiemus ergo thesaurum nostrum, monstrabimus in capitulo 2 exemplo idoneo nonnulla praecepta conformationis signorum deminutae, et tandem exspectabimus hilariter proximam undam.

Pende laxe, Mutabor

PREFACE

1,000 days after publication of our first book, here we are again. We are pleased to present »Lingua Universalis«, featuring 1,301 new icons from our icon workshop. Over this 1,000-day period, in other words, we have created an average of 1.3 icons a day, which we now present to you in what we hope is an appropriate format.

The 1,360 icons contained in »Lingua Grafica« set a benchmark that we thought would not be surpassed that easily. And yet, after the book came out, something happened that, as communication professionals, we should perhaps have anticipated. The first-generation icons and the success of the book released a veritable flood of new pictograms.

Allow us to take this opportunity to thank the many fans of the book, and interested observers. Above all, of course, our thanks go to those who saw »Lingua Grafica« as an invitation to order icons or commission us to develop something new. A heartfelt thanks also, of course, to the pirates out there for helping to disseminate our particular design style.

We are very pleased to present this completely new update: matured in style, sparkling with new content and stuffed full, thanks to busy »clickers«. Pictograms are more relevant today than ever before: they are encroaching on more and more areas that have traditionally been the preserve of the word. Wherever content needs to be understood in a range of languages but there is little room for words, and where complex content can be described more effectively and faster in picture form, these little symbols are appearing.

Whereas in the past icons were found largely in the areas of security, warnings, orientation (not just spatial, but also on the web and other screen applications), today they are being used increasingly to describe, explain and emotionalize (in product presentation, textual environments, on packaging or even the product itself). And this new market is giving birth to new graphic forms. Symbols that widely understandable are now gaining a new character, being varied over and again, and are subject to visual influences such as the graphic guidelines of a given corporate design.

Icon creation today is, therefore, about so much more than simply reducing a message to image form. It is about the form and style of the icon itself. An »icon identity« emerges from the lines in the icon, the relation-ship of black and white areas, the complexity of the whole. The form design says a lot about its origin, the designer or the communication environment in which it will be deployed. »Lingua Universalis« shows both sides: icons that bear the unmistakable hand of Mutabor and those that have shed that mark of origin to adapt to a given environment.

And so, we open our box of treasures once more to reveal in Chapter 2 certain principles of reduced icon creation, with reference to a suitable example, and look forward with excited anticipation to the next wave ...

Hang loose, Mutabor

1000 Tage nach Erscheinen unseres ersten Buches ist es so weit: Wir präsentieren »Lingua Universalis« mit 1301 neuen Icons aus eigener Schmiede. In dem beschriebenen Zeitraum sind also durchschnittlich 1,3 Icons pro Tag in unserem Hause entstanden, die hier nun ihre angemessene Präsentationsfläche finden.

Mit der Zahl von 1360 Icons in »Lingua Grafica« sollte eigentlich eine Marke erreicht werden, die nicht so schnell einzuholen ist. Aber nach Erscheinen des ersten Buches passierte etwas, das man als Kommunikationsprofi eigentlich hätte erwarten müssen. Die Iconwelle der ersten Generation und der Erfolg des Buches lösten eine wahre Flut von neuen Piktogrammen aus.

Den zahlreichen Fans des Buches, den Interessenten und Betrachtern sei an dieser Stelle noch einmal herzlich gedankt. Vor allem natürlich denjenigen, die »Lingua Grafica« als Aufforderung verstanden haben, Icons zu bestellen oder Neuentwicklungen in Auftrag zu geben. Den vielen Raubkopierern möchten wir nur insofern danken, als dass sie dazu beitragen, einen bestimmten Designstil zu verbreiten.

Stilistisch gereift, durch neue Inhalte angeregt und von fleißigen »Klickern« genährt präsentieren wir nun das vollständige Update. Piktogramme sind aktueller denn je, sie dringen in Bereiche vor, die traditionell dem Wort vorbehalten waren. Überall dort, wo Inhalte in unterschiedlichen Sprachen verstanden werden müssen, wo kein Platz ist für viele Worte und sich die Komplexität eines Inhaltes durch ein Bild schneller und besser beschreiben lässt, tauchen die kleinen Zeichen auf.

Kannten wir Icons in der Vergangenheit aus den Bereichen Sicherheit, Warnung, Orientierung (nicht nur im Raum, sondern vor allem auch im Web und anderen Screenanwendungen), dienen sie heute immer mehr der Beschreibung, Erklärung und Emotionalisierung (in der Produktinszenierung, im redaktionellen Umfeld, auf Verpackungen oder am Produkt selbst). Dieser neue Markt führt zu neuen grafischen Formen. Zeichen, die für jedermann verständlich sind, bekommen einen eigenen Charakter, werden immer wieder neu variiert und unterwerfen sich visuellen Strömungen wie z.B. den grafischen Richtlinien eines Corporate Designs.

So geht es bei der Icongestaltung heute um mehr als die reduzierte, bildhafte Botschaft. Es geht um die Form und den Stil des Icons. Eine »Icon-Identität« wird von der Linienführung des Icons, dem Verhältnis von Schwarz- und Weißflächen und der Komplexität geprägt. Die formale Gestaltung sagt viel über seine Herkunft, über den Designer oder das kommunikative Einsatzgebiet. »Lingua Universalis« zeigt beide Seiten: Icons, die die Handschrift von Mutabor tragen, und Icons, die sich der Handschrift entledigt haben und einem wie auch immer gearteten Umfeld angepasst sind.

Wir machen unsere Schatzkiste also erneut auf, zeigen in Kapitel 2 einige Grundsätze der reduzierten Icongestaltung an einem geeigneten Beispiel und freuen uns auf die nächste Flut ...

Hang loose, Mutabor

1000 jours après la parution de notre premier livre, nous sommes prêts : nous présentons »Lingua Universalis« avec 1301 nouvelles icônes de notre cru. Au cours de la période décrite, notre maison a donné naissance à 1,3 icône par jour en moyenne, qui trouvent ici désormais un support de présentation adapté.

Avec le chiffre de 1360 icônes dans »Lingua Grafica« on devrait en fait obtenir une marque qui ne sera pas égalée de sitôt. Or, après la parution du premier livre, il s'est passé ce à quoi un professionnel de la com-munication aurait en fait dû s'attendre. La vague des icônes de la première génération et le succès du livre ont déclenché un véritable flot de nouveaux pictogrammes.

Nous aimerions remercier ici une fois encore chaleureusement les nombreux fans du livre, les personnes intéressées et les observateurs. Et surtout, bien sûr, tous ceux qui ont compris »Lingua Grafica« comme une invitation à réserver des icônes ou à passer commande pour les nouveautés. Sur ce point, nous voudrions remercier les nombreux copieurs pirates, dans la mesure où ils ont contribué à diffuser un certain style de design.

Nous vous présentons aujourd'hui la mise à jour intégrale, avec son style arrivé à maturité, stimulée par de nouveaux contenus et alimentée par les créateurs d'icônes assidus. Les pictogrammes sont plus que jamais au goût du jour et se frayent un chemin dans les domaines traditionnellement consacrés à la communication linguistique. Les petits symboles apparaissent toujours là où des contenus doivent être compris en différentes langues, où la place manque et où une image décrit plus rapidement et bien mieux la complexité d'un contenu.

Autrefois, nous connaissions les icônes dans les domaines de la sécurité, pour avertir, pour s'orienter (non seulement dans des locaux, mais surtout également sur Internet et pour d'autres applications sur écran); aujourd'hui, elles servent de plus en plus à décrire, expliquer et passionner (dans la mise en scène d'un produit, dans un environnement rédactionnel, sur les emballages ou sur le produit lui-même).

Ce nouveau marché amène de nouvelles formes graphiques. Les symboles, compréhensibles pour tous, reçoivent un caractère propre, sont modifiés à l'infini et soumis à des courants visuels, par exemple aux directives graphiques d'un design collectif.

Ainsi, la réalisation d'une icône va aujourd'hui bien au-delà du message abrégé et imagé. Il s'agit de la forme et du style de l'icône. »L'identité de l'icône« est marquée par le tracé de l'icône, par la proportion de surfaces noires et blanches et par la complexité. La réalisation formelle en dit long sur son origine, son créateur ou le domaine d'application communicatif. »Lingua Universalis« dévoile les deux facettes : les icônes qui portent la griffe de Mutabor, et les icônes qui s'en sont libérées, s'adaptant à un environnement différent quel qu'il soit.

Nous ouvrons donc de nouveau notre malle aux trésors, indiquons au chapitre 2 quelques principes de la réalisation d'une icône abrégée par un exemple adapté et attendons le prochain flot avec impatience ...

Hang loose, Mutabor

PRÓLOGO

Tras 1000 días de la publicación de nuestro primer libro presentamos ahora »Lingua Universalis« con 1301 iconos nuevos de cuña propia. Durante este periodo hemos creado un promedio de 1,3 iconos al día que hallarán aquí su plataforma de presentación correspondiente.

Con la cifra de 1360 iconos, pensábamos que »Lingua Grafica« había establecido una marca que no se alcanza tan fácilmente. Sin embargo, después de la publicación del primer libro ha ocurrido algo que como expertos en comunicación en realidad tendríamos que haber previsto. La ola de iconos de la primera generación y el éxito del libro provocaron un verdadero diluvio de nuevos pictogramas.

Aprovechamos esta ocasión para agradecer su interés a los numerosos admiradores del libro, interesados y lectores. Y especialmente a aquellos que han entendido »Lingua Grafica« como una invitación a hacer sus pedidos de iconos o encomendar uno nuevo. Queremos dar nuestro sincero agradecimiento a los muchos copiadores ilegales por haber colaborado en la divulgación de un determinado estilo de diseño.

Presentamos ahora la actualización completa, estilísticamente más madura, con el estímulo de un nuevo contenido y desarrollada con la ayuda de colaboradores aplicados. Los pictogramas son ahora más importantes que nunca. Se internan en sectores que tradicionalmente estaban reservados a la palabra. Los pequeños símbolos emergen en todas partes donde los contenidos deben entenderse en diferentes idiomas, donde no hay lugar para muchas palabras y donde resulta más rápido y mejor describir la complejidad de un contenido mediante una imagen.

Antes conocíamos iconos en los campos de seguridad, advertencia, orientación (no sólo en el espacio, sino sobre todo en Internet y otras aplicaciones de pantalla), pero hoy día sirven cada vez más como descripción, explicación y como signos emotivos (en la presentación de productos, en el entorno editorial, en envases
o en los mismos productos). Este nuevo mercado conduce a nuevos formas gráficas. Signos que son entendidos por todos, adquieren su propio carácter, se pueden volver a modificar y son sometidos a corrientes visuales, como por ejemplo las líneas gráficas de un diseño corporativo.

Por estos motivos, diseñar un icono hoy día implica más que crear un mensaje reducido y figurativo. Todo gira en torno a la forma y al estilo del icono. La »identidad del icono« está determinada por la dirección de sus líneas, la relación entre las superficies blancas y negras y la complejidad. El diseño formal dice mucho sobre su origen, el diseñador o el campo comunicativo de uso. »Lingua Universalis« muestra ambos lados: iconos que llevan la firma de Mutabor e iconos que prescinden de ella para adaptarse a un determinado campo, sea cual sea su naturaleza.

Así que de nuevo abrimos nuestro joyero mostrando en el capítulo 2 algunos axiomas de la creación de iconos reducidos con un ejemplo apropiado y alegrándonos del diluvio que está al caer...

Hang loose, Mutabor

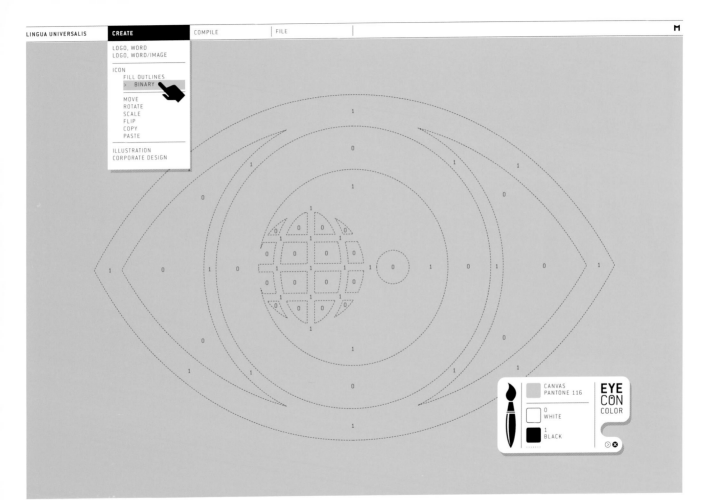

020 > 045
WORKSHOP

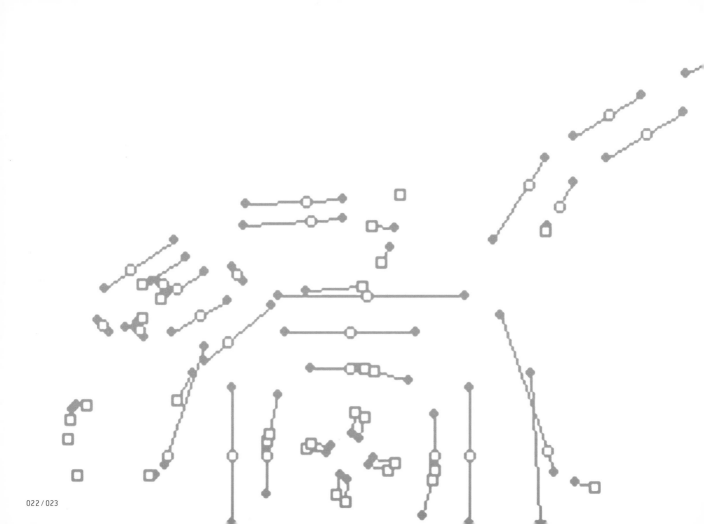

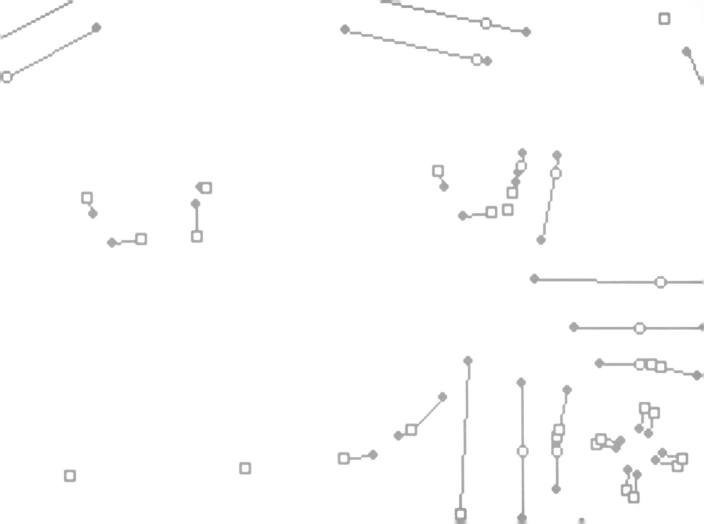

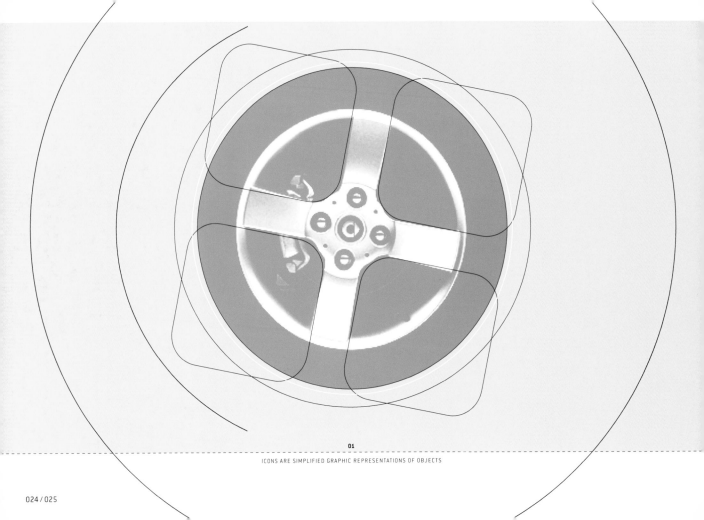

01

ICONS ARE SIMPLIFIED GRAPHIC REPRESENTATIONS OF OBJECTS

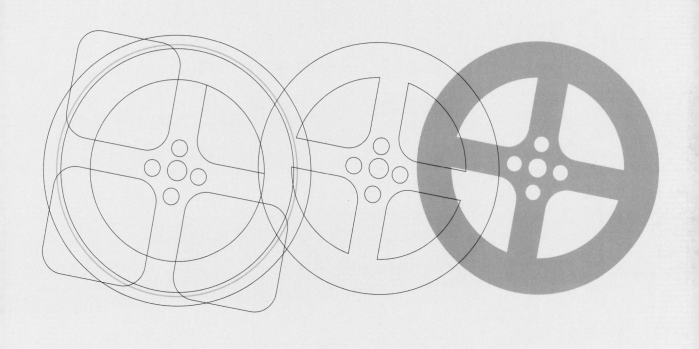

SIMPLIFICATION IN GRAPHICS IS BASED ON BASIC GEOMETRIC SHAPES

LINGUA UNIVERSALIS

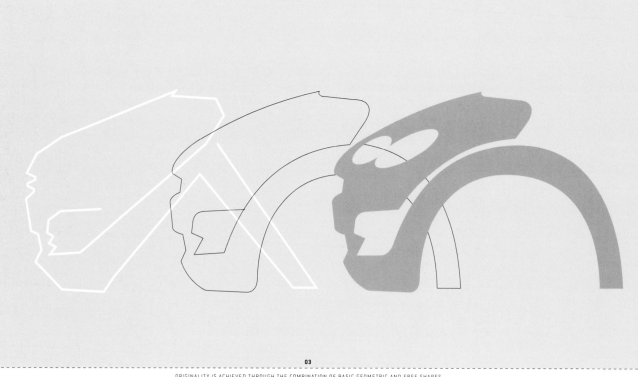

ORIGINALITY IS ACHIEVED THROUGH THE COMBINATION OF BASIC GEOMETRIC AND FREE SHAPES

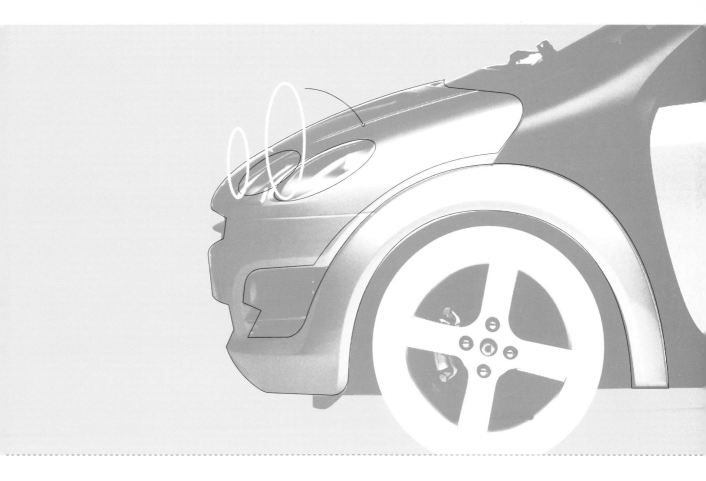

AN OBJECT IS CREATED BY COMBINING FREE AND BASIC SHAPES

LINGUA UNIVERSALIS

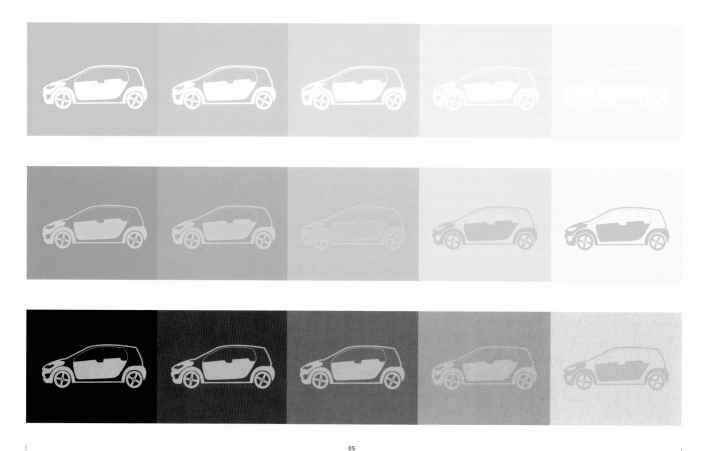

OBJECTS ACHIEVE THEIR OWN EFFECT THROUGH COLORATION

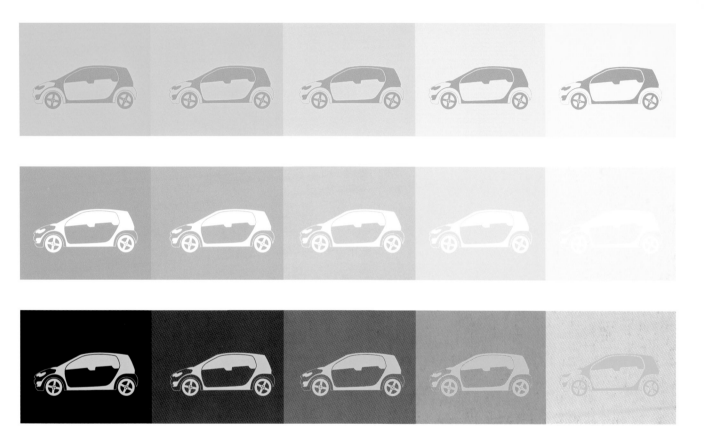

THE COLORATION FOLLOWS THE PLAY OF POSITIVE AND NEGATIVE SHAPES

07

THE ACTUAL SHAPE DEPENDS ON THE SIZE OF THE PICTURE

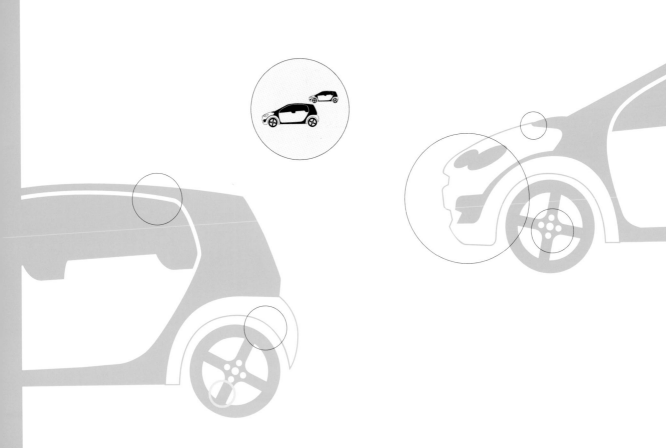

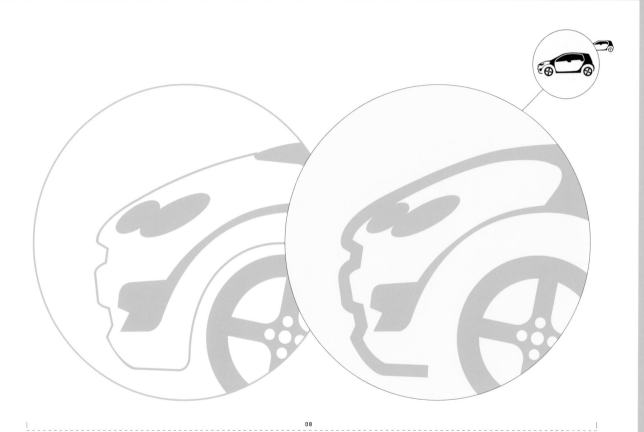

THE PICTURE SIZE DETERMINES THE COMPLEXITY OF THE LINE DIRECTION

LINGUA UNIVERSALIS

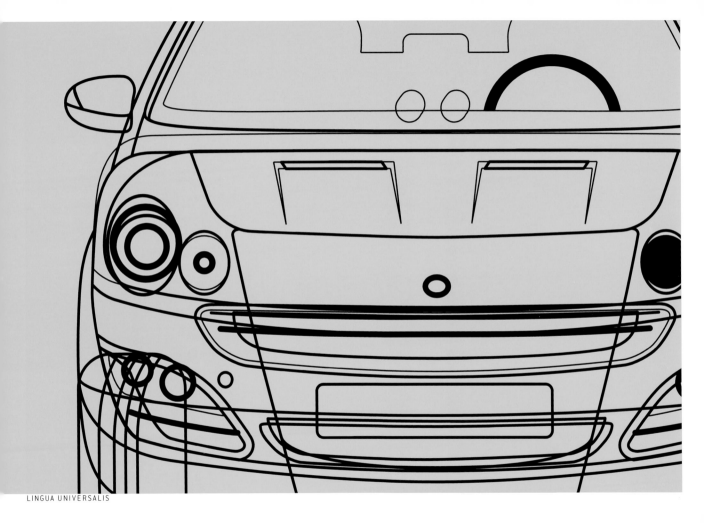

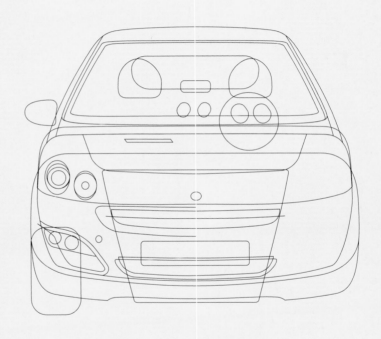

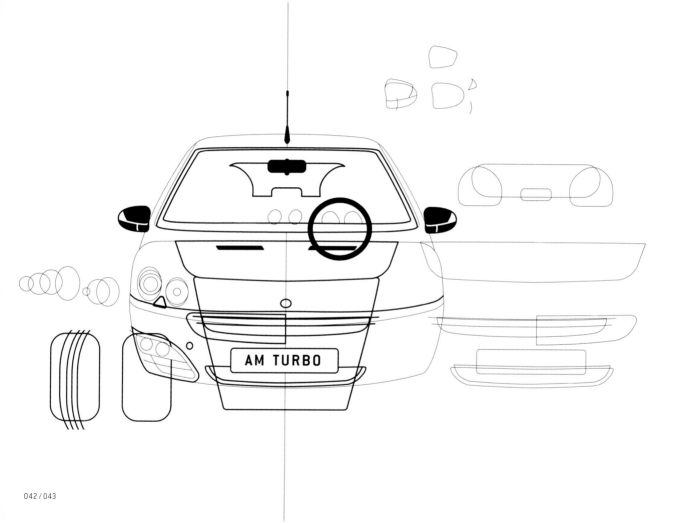

AM TURBO

AM TURBO

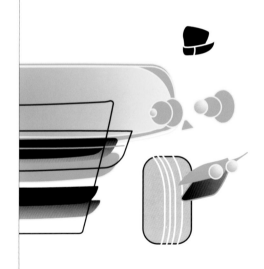

BY: NAME
BY: NUMBER

BY: CLIENT
LINGUA UNIVERSALIS
> 1361

CLASSEN-PAPIE
CORE MEDIA
DIVERSE
FACEPARTY
GREENPEACE
MUTABOR X
PREMIUM

01_RZ EYE

ART:
FREEHAND 9 DOKUMENT

GROESSE:
24 KB (18.754 BYTES)

ORT:
JOBS 2: PROJEKTE: BÜCHER:
LINGUA UNIVERSALIS: RZ

ERSTELLT:
DIE, 8. JUL 2003, 18:36 UHR

VERSION:
15

046 > 181
CATALOGUE

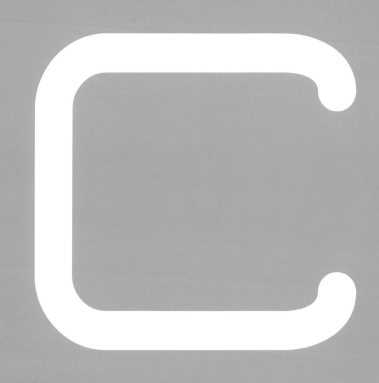

1362 > 1364
CLASSEN-PAPIER, CLIENTS
- ->

1365 > 1368
CLASSEN-PAPIER, X-MAS
- ->

1362	1363	1364	1365
DESIGNER	PRODUCER	PRINTER	

1369 > 1375
CLASSEN-PAPIER, BUSINESS
- ->

1366	1367	1368	1369	1370

1371	1372	1373	1374	1375

Beispiel®
by CLASSEN

1376

Gainsborough
by CLASSEN

1377

Granuprint®
by CLASSEN

1378

figaro
by CLASSEN

1379

Himalaya
by CLASSEN

1380

SYNTEAPE
by CLASSEN

1381

Fanfare
by CLASSEN

1382

Fuego®
Premium Paper by CLASSEN

1383

Noblesse®
Premium Paper by CLASSEN

1384

Classen Classifier
Gesamtübersicht

1385

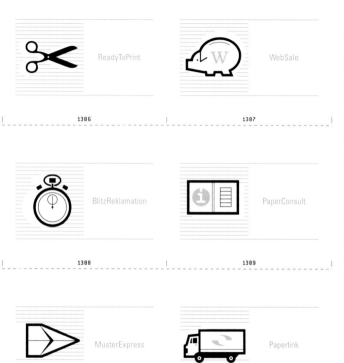

ReadyToPrint

1386

WebSale

1387

BlitzReklamation

1388

PaperConsult

1389

MusterExpress

1390

Paperlink

1391

1392

Sonne

Erde

Mond

1394

LUNAR ECLIPSE

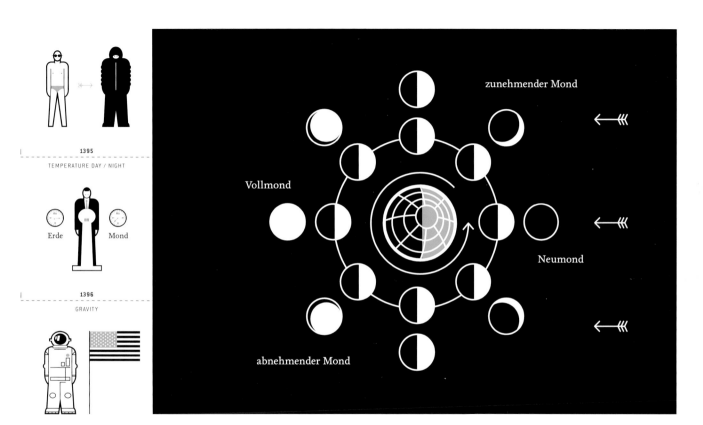

1395

TEMPERATURE DAY / NIGHT

Erde   Mond

1396

GRAVITY

1397

HISTORY

zunehmender Mond

Vollmond

Neumond

abnehmender Mond

1398

PHASES OF THE MOON

1399	1400	1401	1402	1403	1404	1405
SILK	GLOSS	GLOSS	PREPRINT	PREPRINT	OFFSET	OFFSET

1406	1407	1408	1409	1410	1411	1412	1413
BULK	BULK	RECYCLING	RECYCLING	RECYCLING	RECYCLING	NATURAL	NATURAL

1414	1415	1416	1417	1418	1419	1420	1421
COLOR	COLOR	CARTON	CARTON	OFFICE	OFFICE	DIGITAL	DIGITAL

1422	1423	1424	1425	1426	1427	1428	1429
MAIL	MAIL	SD	SD	TECHNICAL	TECHNICAL	SPECIAL	SPECIAL

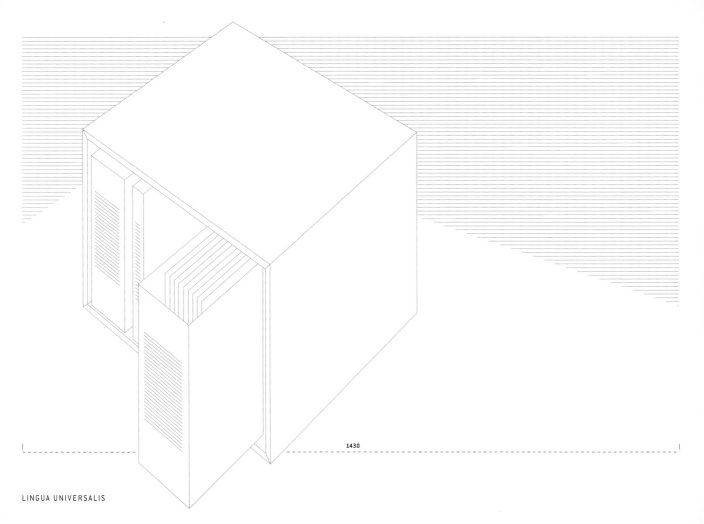

1430

LINGUA UNIVERSALIS

1431	1432	1433	1434	1435
PHOTOCOPIER	INKJET PRINTER	FAX	LASER PRINTER	AMOUNT OF SHEETS

1436	1437	1438	1439	1440	1441	1442	1443
B/W INKJET	INKJET	LASER	COLOR LASER	COPY	COLOR COPY	DUPLEX COPY	PRINTABLE SIDE

1444	1445	1446	1447	1448	1449	1450	1451
BOTH SIDED	ONE SIDED	WATERPROOF	WEAR RESISTANT	UV-RESISTANT	TEMPERATURE	4x PUNCHED	2x PUNCHED

TCF	720	2880	1440	4800
1452	1453	1454	1455	1456
CHLORINE FREE	720 DPI	1440 DPI	2880 DPI	4800 DPI

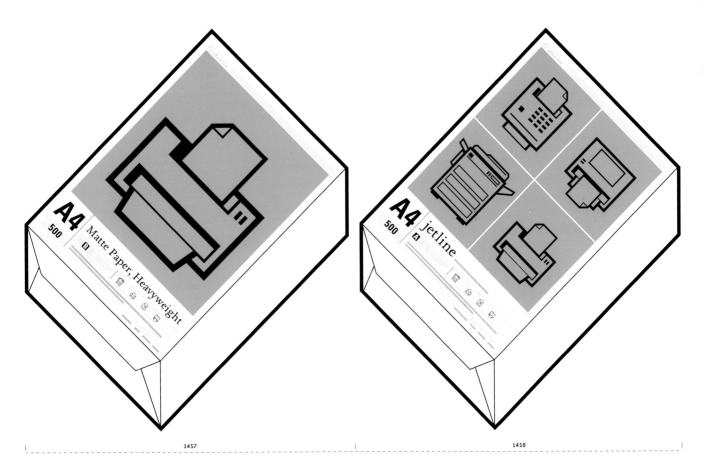

A4
500 · Matte Paper, Heavyweight

A4
500 · jetline

1457   1458

1459 > 1472
CLASSEN-PAPIER, PHASE 2 (DETAIL)

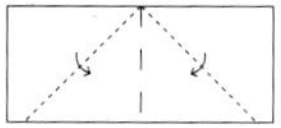

1459

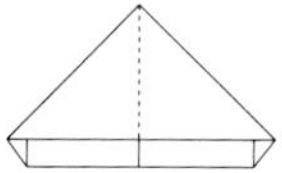

1460

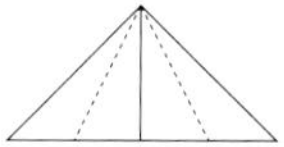

1461

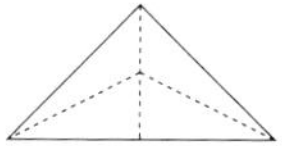

1462

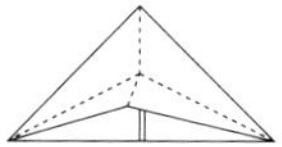

1463

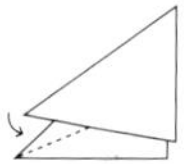

1464

1465

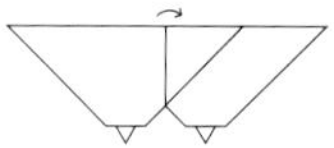

1466

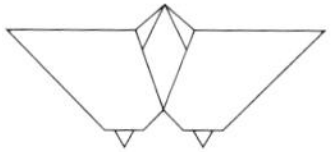

1467

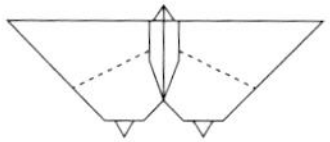

1468

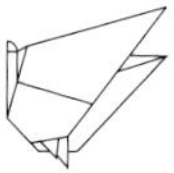

1469

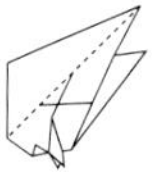

1470

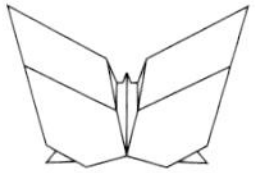

1471

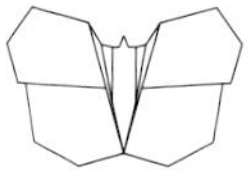

1472

1473 > 1477
CLASSEN-PAPIER, DESK PAD 2002

1473

1478 > 1482
CLASSEN-PAPIER, DESK PAD 2003

1483 > 1484
CLASSEN-PAPIER, FUEGO

1478

SHOULDER CIRCLING

1474

1475

1479

SIGNPOST

1480

FINGER-WRESTLING

1483

1476

1477

1481

ROPE-LADDER

1482

EAGLE

1484

CHEERS!

1485 > 1630 CORE MEDIA

MCF MEDIACORE (MUTABOR CUSTOMIZED FONT)

1485	1486	1487	1488	1489	1490	1491
ALIGN CENTER	ALIGN JUSTIFY	ALIGN LEFT	ALIGN NONE	ALIGN RIGHT	PARAGRAPH FORMAT	TEXT ALIGNMENT
1492	1493	1494	1495	1496	1497	1498	1499
INDENT	LIST BULLET	LIST NUMBERED	LISTS	OUTDENT	SUBSCRIPT	SUPERSCRIPT	BOLD
1500	1501	1502	1503	1504	1505	1506	1507
ITALIC	FONT NAME	FONT SIZE	TEXT COLOR	TEXT FORMAT	SELECT FONT	UNDERLINE	STRIKE
1508	1509	1510	1511	1512	1513	1514	1515
ADD COLUMN	ADD ROW	REMOVE COLUMN	REMOVE ROW	INSERT COLUMN	INSERT COLUMNS	INSERT COLUMN RIGHT	INSERT ROW

1516	1517	1518	1519	1520	1521	1522	1523
INSERT ROWS	INSERT ROW BELOW	SPLIT CELLS	MERGE CELLS VERTICAL	REMOVE CELLCONTENT			

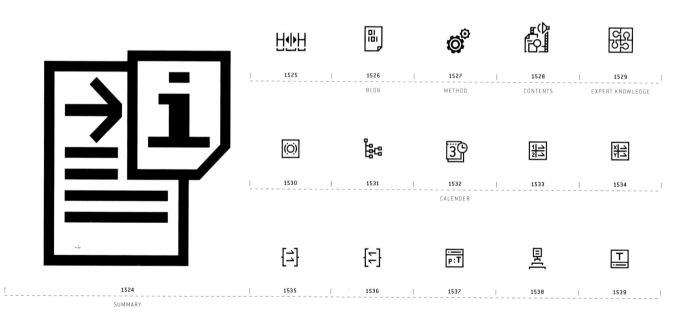

1525	1526	1527	1528	1529
	BLOB	METHOD	CONTENTS	EXPERT KNOWLEDGE

1530	1531	1532	1533	1534
		CALENDER		

1524
SUMMARY

1535	1536	1537	1538	1539

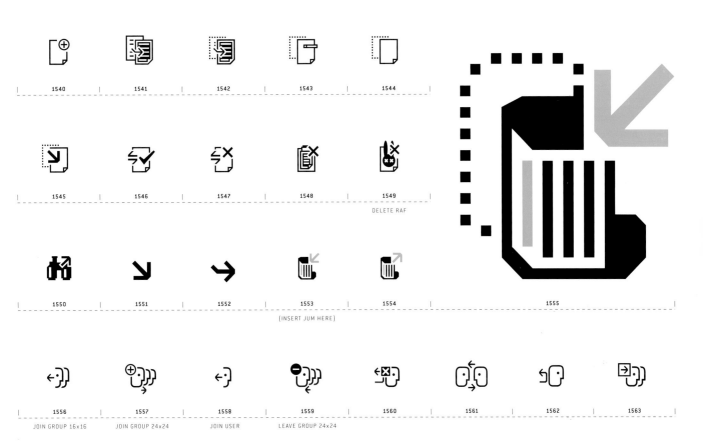

1540

1541

1542

1543

1544

1545

1546

1547

1548

1549

DELETE RAF

1550

1551

1552

1553

1554

1555

(INSERT JUM HERE)

1556

1557

1558

1559

1560

1561

1562

1563

JOIN GROUP 16x16

JOIN GROUP 24x24

JOIN USER

LEAVE GROUP 24x24

| 1564 | 1565 | 1566 | 1567 | 1568 | 1569 | 1570 | 1571 |

| 1572 | 1573 | 1574 | 1575 | 1576 | 1577 | 1578 | 1579 |

| 1580 | 1581 | 1582 | 1583 | 1584 | 1585 | 1586 | 1587 |
| ESCALATION | TASK | COMPLETE PROCESS | ESCALATED TASK | INSERT IMAGE | SGML TEXT | ABORT PROCESS | ALL DOC TYPES |

| 1588 | 1589 | 1590 | 1591 | 1592 | 1593 | 1594 | 1595 |
| LINK LIST | DICT ENTRY | MAGNIFIER | | | PROCESS | WORKFLOW | OPEN TASK |

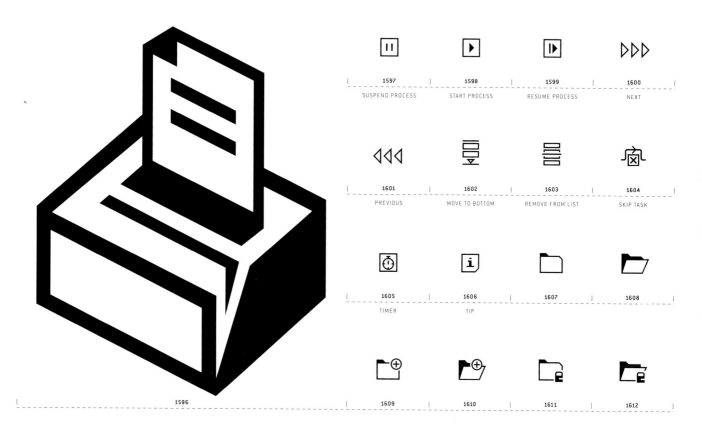

1597	1598	1599	1600
SUSPEND PROCESS	START PROCESS	RESUME PROCESS	NEXT
1601	1602	1603	1604
PREVIOUS	MOVE TO BOTTOM	REMOVE FROM LIST	SKIP TASK
1605	1606	1607	1608
TIMER	TIP		
1609	1610	1611	1612

1596

1613	1614	1615	1616	1617	1618	1619	1620

1621	1622	1623	1624	1625	1626	1627	1628

1629	1630
WARNING	[END LIST]

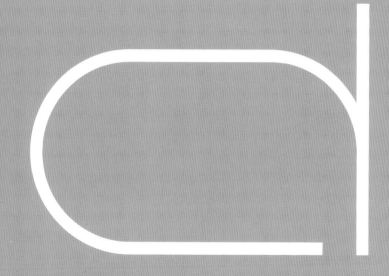

MCF STRIPE (MUTABOR CUSTOMIZED FONT)

1631

NEW!

1632

MUSIC

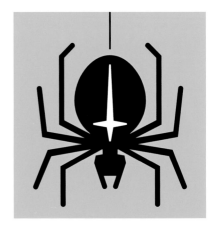

1636

HORROR

1633

ROMANCE

1634

ADULT ENTERTAINMENT

1635

SCIENCE FICTION

1637

RELAXATION

1638

SUSPENSE

1639

BIG EMOTIONS

1640

ACTION

1641

FUN

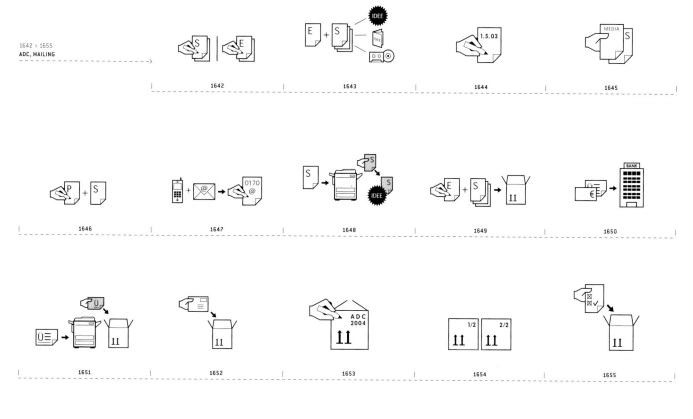

1656 > 1676
ARTGENDA 2002, HAMBURG

1656
OPENING

1657
LOUNGE

1658
HALL OF FAME

1659
BUYING / SELLING

1660
FOOD / DRINK

1661
CHILLOUT

1662
INDOOR

1663
OUTDOOR

1664
CITY OFFICIALS ARE PRESENT

1665
GUIDED TOUR

1666
VERY PHOTOGENIC

1667
EXHIBITION

1668
MUSIC / PARTY

1669
FILM / TV / VIDEO

1670
PERFORMANCE / THEATRE / CONCERT

1671
INSTALLATION

1672
DISCUSSION / SYMPOSIUM

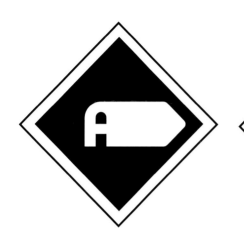

1673

1

1674

2

1675

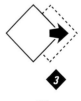

3

1676

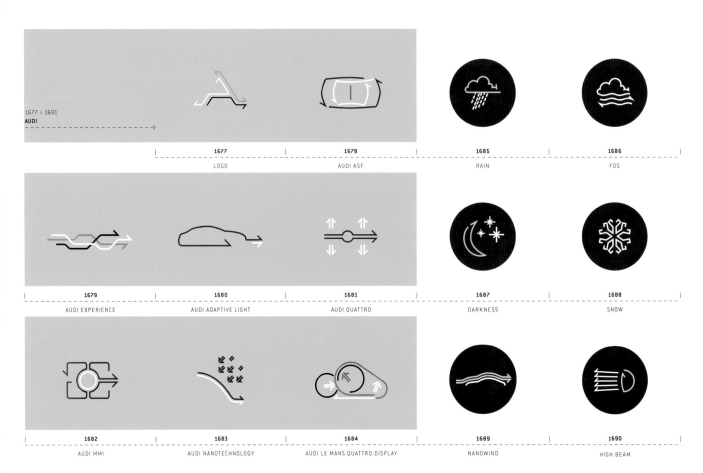

1677 > 1691
AUDI

| 1677 | 1678 | 1685 | 1686 |
| LOGO | AUDI ASF | RAIN | FOG |

| 1679 | 1680 | 1681 | 1687 | 1688 |
| AUDI EXPERIENCE | AUDI ADAPTIVE LIGHT | AUDI QUATTRO | DARKNESS | SNOW |

| 1682 | 1683 | 1684 | 1689 | 1690 |
| AUDI MMI | AUDI NANOTECHNOLOGY | AUDI LE MANS QUATTRO DISPLAY | NANOWIND | HIGH BEAM |

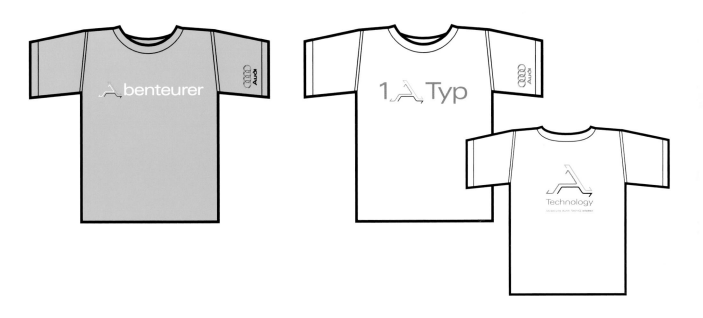

LINGUA UNIVERSALIS

1692 > 1704
BEISNER DRUCK - - - - - - - - - - - - - - - - - ->

1692

D.I.Y. X-MAS TREE 1

1693

D.I.Y. X-MAS TREE 2

1694

D.I.Y. X-MAS TREE 3

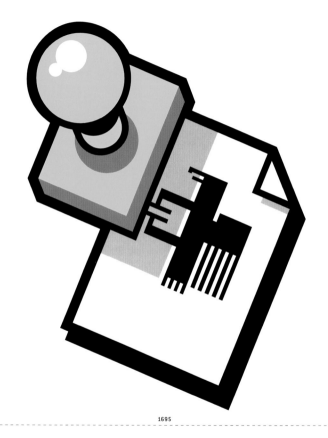

1695

EBV / PROOF

1696

E. I. P. / PROOF

LITHOGRAFIE

1697

LITHOGRAPHY

SIEBDRUCK

1698

SERIGRAPHY

SCHRIFTSATZ

1699

TYPESETTING

GESTALTUNG

1700

DESIGN

AKZIDENZEN

1701

JOB PRINTING

OFFSETDRUCK

1702

OFFSET

BUCHDRUCK

1703

LETTERPRESS

FARBSCAN

1704

COLOR SCAN

1708

| 1705 | 1706 | 1707 |

 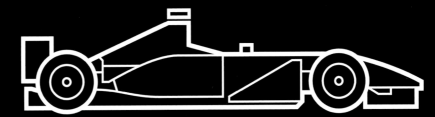

1708

... IS DANGEROUS!

1709 > 1714

BRISKY MEDIA, LOGOTYPE
– →

| 1709 | 1710 |

| 1711 | 1712 | 1713 | 1714 |

1715 > 1729
CYBIRD, 200x200 PX ICON-REMIXES
-------------------------------- ->

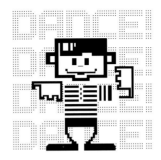
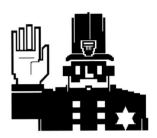

1715		1716		1717	
0389 (REMIX)				0352 (REMIX)	

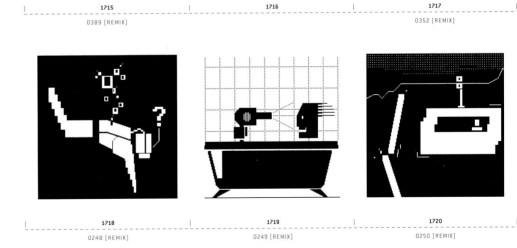

1718		1719		1720	
0248 (REMIX)		0249 (REMIX)		0250 (REMIX)	

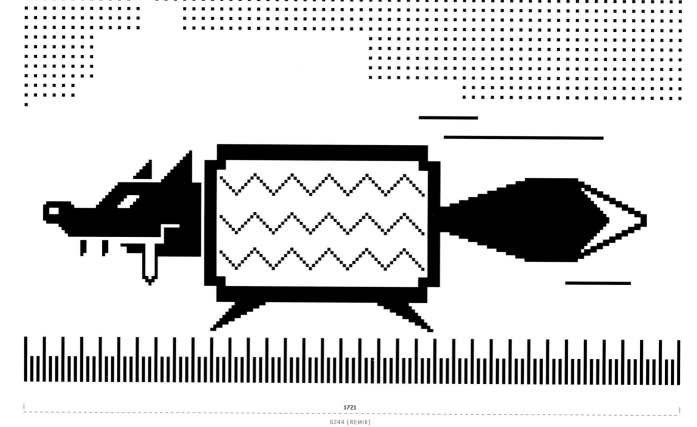

1721

0244 (REMIX)

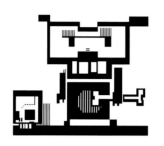

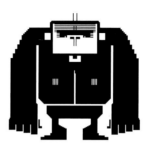

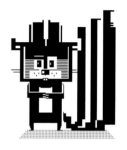

1722	1723	1724	1725
0243 (REMIX)		2585 (REMIX)	0245 (REMIX)

1726	1727	1728	1729
0440 (REMIX)	0435 (REMIX)	0437 (REMIX)	0434 (REMIX)

1730 > 1735
CYBIRD, SUMMERLOVE
- ->

| 1730 | 1731 | 1732 |

1736 > 1737
DAIMINGER INC., KOALA
- ->

| 1733 | 1734 | 1735 |

1736

1737

1747

| 1738 | 1739 | 1740 | 1741 |

| 1742 | 1743 | 1744 | 1745 | 1746 |

MOBILE TV   DIGI.ON DEMAND   DIGI STREAM   WAP MOBILE   MOBILE NEWS

| 1748 | 1749 | 1750 | 1751 | 1752 |

1753 > 1770
FABERCASTELL, LOGO-REDESIGN

1753

1754

1755

1756

1757

1758

1759

1760

1761

1762

1763

1764

1765

1766

1767

1768

1769

1770

1771 > 1805
FETTES BROT, DEMOTAPE / SCHWULE MÄDCHEN →

1771

1772

1779

QUEER SISSY 1

1780

QUEER SISSY 2

1773

1774

1775

1781

QUEER SISSY 2

1782

QUEER SISSIES

1776

1777

1778

1783

QUEER SISSIES

1784

QUEER SISSIES

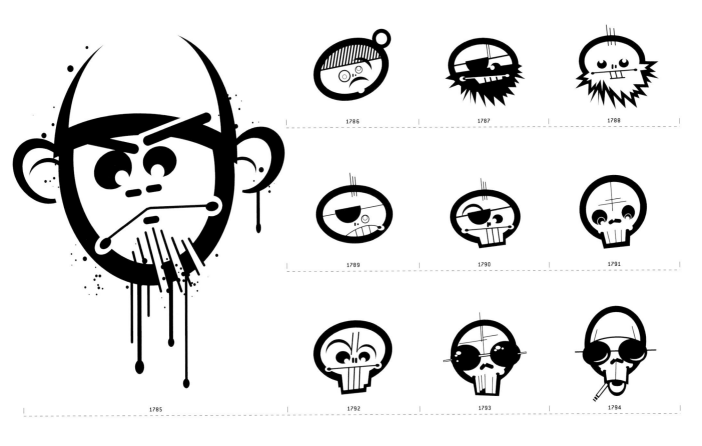

1785

1786 1787 1788

1789 1790 1791

1792 1793 1794

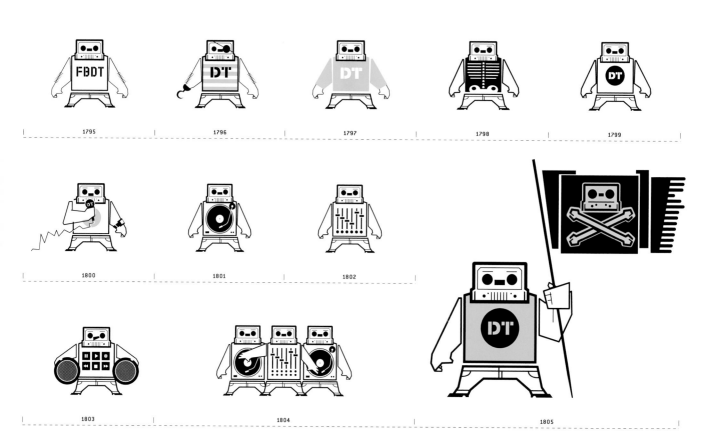

1795

1796

1797

1798

1799

1800

1801

1802

1803

1804

1805

foodwatch®

1806

1807

FOOD WATCH

1808

1809

1810 > 1824
GO!RILLA, LOGOTYPE
- - - - - - - - - - - - - - ->

1810

1811

1812

1813

1814

1815

1816

1817

1818

1819

1820

1821

1822

1823

1824

1825	1826	1827
YUL BRYNER	STEVE MCQUEEN	HORST BUCHHOLZ

1828	1829	1830	1831
BRAD DEXTER	CHARLES BRONSON	JAMES COBURN	ROBERT VAUGHN

1832

1833

1834

1835

1836

1837

1838

1839

1840

1841

1843

1844

1845

1846

1847

1848

1849

1850

1851

1852

1853

1854

1855

1856

1857

ODDSET / TOTO

1858

ALL IN ONE

1859

CASINO

1860

1861

1862

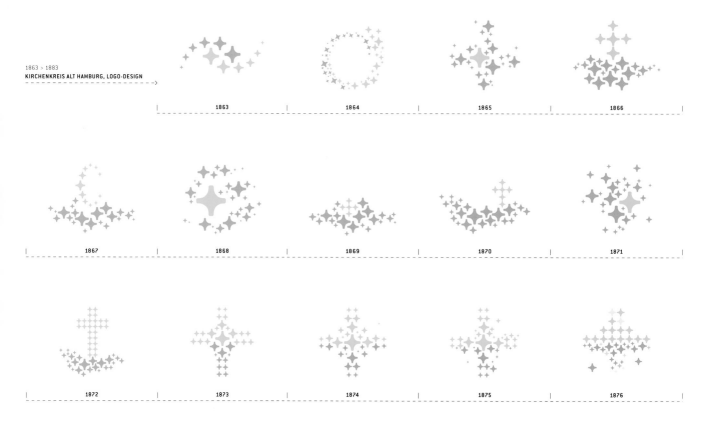

1863   1864   1865   1866

1867   1868   1869   1870   1871

1872   1873   1874   1875   1876

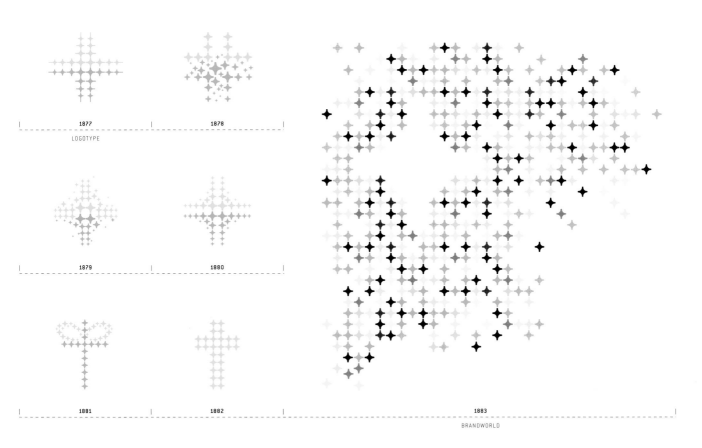

1877

1878

1879

1880

1881

1882

1883

BRANDWORLD

LINGUA UNIVERSALIS

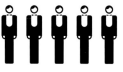

1884   1885   1886   1887   1888

1889   1890   1891   1892   1893   1894   1895   1896

1897   1898   1899   1900   1901   1902   1903   1904

1905   1906   1907   1908   1909   1910   1911   1912

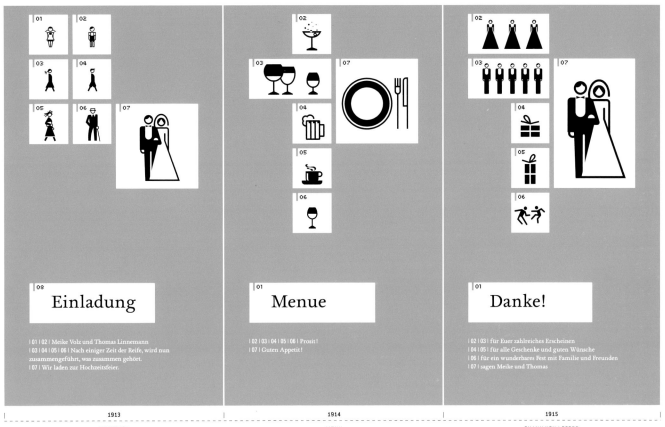

08	**Einladung**

| 01 | 02 | Meike Volz und Thomas Linnemann
| 03 | 04 | 05 | 06 | Nach einiger Zeit der Reife, wird nun zusammengeführt, was zusammen gehört.
| 07 | Wir laden zur Hochzeitsfeier.

01	**Menue**

| 02 | 03 | 04 | 05 | 06 | Prosit!
| 07 | Guten Appetit!

01	**Danke!**

| 02 | 03 | für Euer zahlreiches Erscheinen
| 04 | 05 | für alle Geschenke und guten Wünsche
| 06 | für ein wunderbares Fest mit Familie und Freunden
| 07 | sagen Meike und Thomas

1916	1917	1918	1919	1920	1921	1922
WIRELESS DEVICES	WIRELESS APPLICATIONS	LONGEVITY OF LIVE	COLLABORATION	ADAPTATION	HUMAN	AD-HOC STORY SYSTEMS

1923	1924	1925	1926	1927	1928	1929	1930
PEOPLE'S BEHAVIOUR	EXPRESSING	SENSORY IMMERSION	SELF ORGANISING SYSTEMS	BIONIC INTIMACY	DIGITAL STORIES	STORIES FOR PUBLIC PLACES	INTERACTION

1931	1932	1933	1934	1935	1936	1937	1938
INTERCULTURAL COMMUNICATION	OPEN MINDED	APPROPRIATING	CONNECTEDNESS	HUMAN INSTINCT	CONTEXT-AWARE MEDIA	INTERCULTURAL BONDS	TECHNOLOGY

1939	1940	1941	1942	1943	1944	1945	1946
CONVERGENCE	CONNECTEDNESS	MACHINE	AWARENESS	NARRATIVES	SPEECH BASED	BIOMETRICS	TECHNOLOGY AS A CATALYST

1947

COMMUNITY

1948

HUMAN COMPUTER

1949

TECHNOLOGICAL FRAMEWORK

1950

CREATION

1951

MUSIC TOYS

1952

MOBILE COMMUNICATION

1953

POINT OF VIEW NARRATIVES

1954

MOBILE NARRATIVES

1955

DECENTRALISED SYSTEMS

1956

BIOSYNTHESIS

1957

INTERACTION THROUGH TOUCH

1958 > 1966
MLE, ICON-ILLUSTRATIONS
- - - - - - - - - - - - - - - - - - >

COLLABORATION

COMMUNITY

AWARENESS

CONNECTEDNES

TECHNOLOGICAL FRAMEWORK

1958

HUMAN CONNECTEDNESS

LINGUA UNIVERSALIS

INTERACTION

SPEECH BASED INTERFACES

INTERCULTURAL BONDS

1959

ADAPTIVE SPEECH INTERFACES

WIRELESS APPLICATIONS

USERS INTERACTION

BIOSYNTHESIS

SELF ORGANISING SYSTEMS

1960

DYNAMIC INTERACTIONS

HAPTIC INTERACTION

INFORMATION THROUGH TOUCH

HUMAN SENSORY SYSTEM

1961

PALPABLE MACHINES

NEW SOUNDS

USERS INTERACTION

MUSIC CREATION

MUSIC TOYS

1962

FUTURE MUSIC

BIOMETRICS

INTELLIGENT BIOFEEDBACK

SENSORY IMMERSION

HUMAN COMPUTER INTERFACE

1963

MINDGAMES

EXPRESSING

APPROPRIATING

ADAPTATION

TECHNOLOGY

1964

EVERYDAY LEARNING

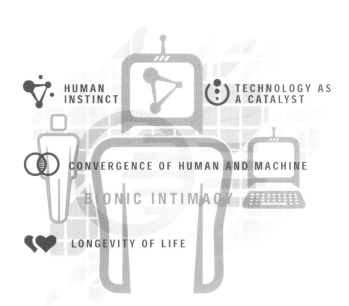

HUMAN
INSTINCT

 TECHNOLOGY AS
A CATALYST

CONVERGENCE OF HUMAN AND MACHINE

BIONIC INTIMACY

LONGEVITY OF LIFE

 AD-HOC STORY
SYSTEMS

CONTEXT-AWARE
MEDIA

MOBILE NARRATIVES

 POINT-OF-VIEW
NARRATIVES

STORIES FOR PUBLIC PLACES

1965	1966
ELIXIR PROJECT	STORY NETWORKS

Naturathlon
2004   NATUR BEWEGT

1967

1968

1969

1970

1971

1972

1973

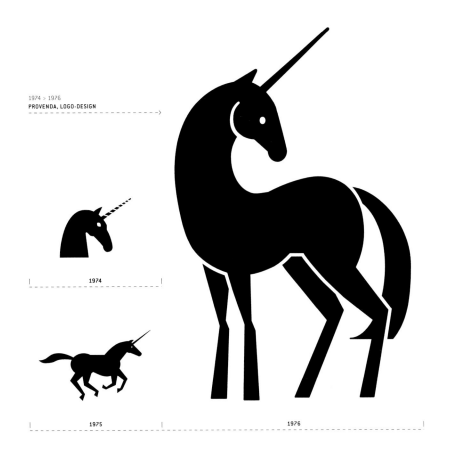

1974

1975

1976

1977

 1978

 1979

 1980

 1981

 1982

 1983

 1984

 1985

1986

1987

 1988

1989

1990

1991

1992

1993

1994

 1995

 1996

 1997

1998

 1999

REA AG | Regenerative Energie Anlagen

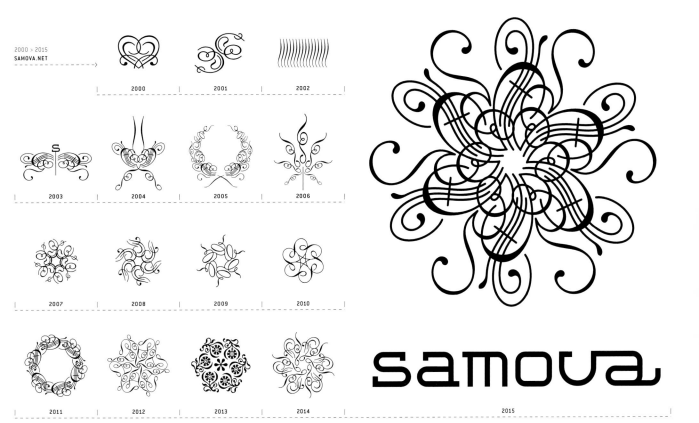

2000

2001

2002

2003

2004

2005

2006

2007

2008

2009

2010

2011

2012

2013

2014

2015

LINGUA UNIVERSALIS

2016

PLUMBING

2017

CUSTOMER SERVICE

2018

SANITARY

2019

HEATING

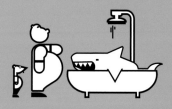

2020

VENTILATION

2021

SANITARY

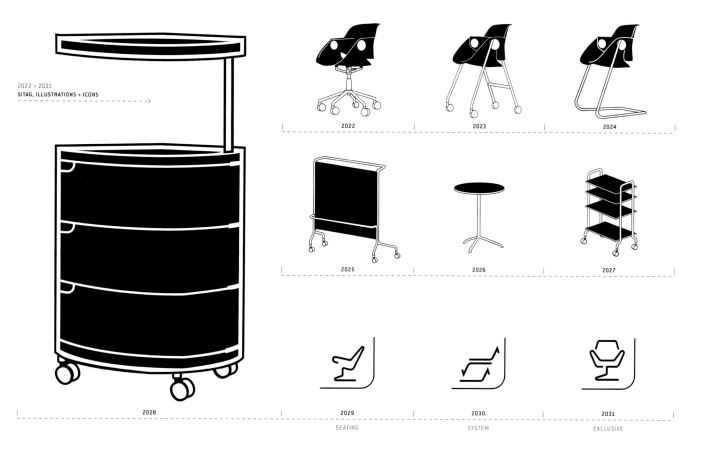

2022 > 2031
SITAG, ILLUSTRATIONS + ICONS

2022

2023

2024

2025

2026

2027

2028

2029

2030

2031

SEATING

SYSTEM

EXCLUSIVE

LINGUA UNIVERSALIS

2032

2033

2034

2035

2036

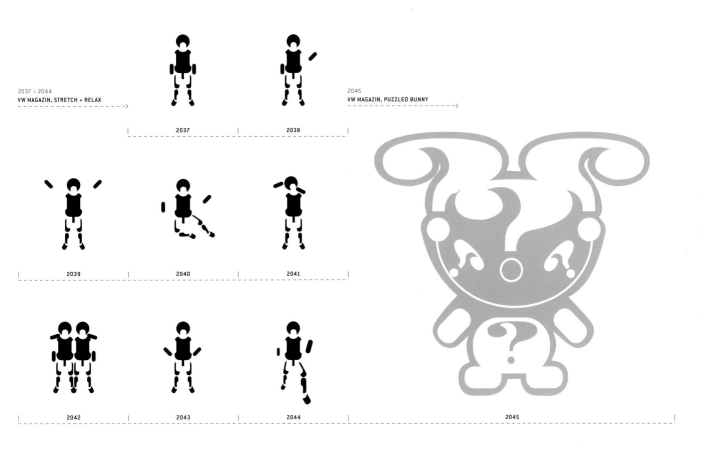

2037 > 2044
VW MAGAZIN, STRETCH + RELAX - - - - - - - ->

2045
VW MAGAZIN, PUZZLED BUNNY - - - - - - - - ->

2037 | 2038

2039 | 2040 | 2041

2042 | 2043 | 2044

2045

2046

CALLCENTER

2047

CALLCENTER

2048

2049

SAND YACHTING

2050

SAND YACHTING

2051

SAND YACHTING

2052

SAND YACHTING

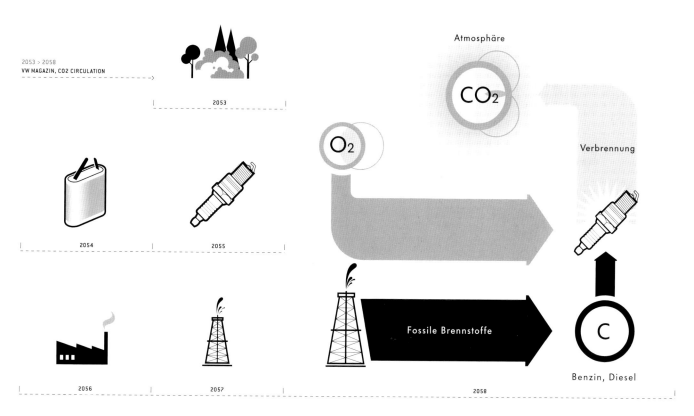

2053

2054

2055

2056

2057

2058

Atmosphäre

CO_2

O_2

Verbrennung

Fossile Brennstoffe

C

Benzin, Diesel

2059 > 2133 FACEPARTY

MCF BÜRO 3000 (MUTABOR CUSTOMIZED FONT)

2059 > 2084
FACEPARTY.COM, GRIM-RITA LOGO-DESIGN
- ->

2059

2060

2061

2062

2063

2064

2065

2066

2067

2068

2069

2070

2071

2072

2073

2074

2075

2076

2077

2078

2079

2080

2081

2082

2083

2084

2085   2086

2087   2088   2089   2090

THE BIGGEST PARTY IN THE WORLD

2091   2092   2093   2094   2095

faceparty

2102

2096

2097

2098

2099

2100

2101

2103

2104

2105   2106   2107   2108

2109   2110   2111   2112

2113 2114

2115

2116

2117

2118

2119

2120

2121

2122

2123

2124

2125

2126

2127

2128

2129

Faceparty

THE BIGGEST PARTY ON EARTH

2130

LOGO, 1 C, POSITIVE

Faceparty

THE BIGGEST PARTY ON EARTH

2131

LOGO, 1 C, NEGATIVE

Faceparty

THE BIGGEST PARTY ON EARTH

2132

LOGO, 3 C

2133

LOGO VARIATION

LINGUA UNIVERSALIS

2134 > 2346 GREENPEACE

MCF DEMOTYPE (MUTABOR CUSTOMIZED FONT)

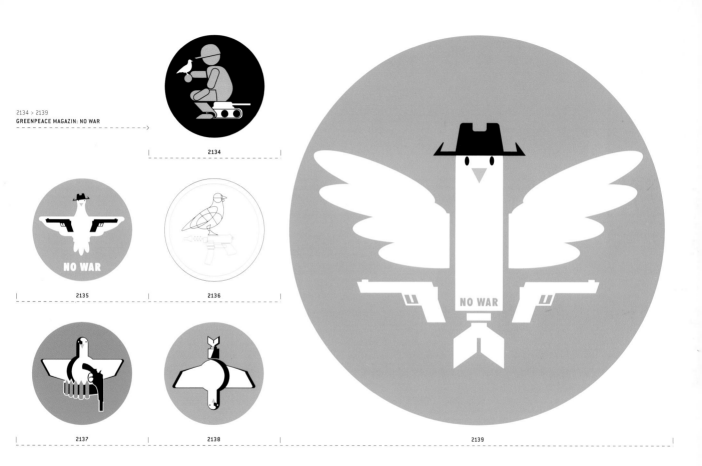

2134 > 2139
GREENPEACE MAGAZIN: NO WAR

2134

2135

2136

2137

2138

2139

NO WAR

2140

ARMED CONFLICT

2141

CIVIL WAR

2142

WAR

2143

PEACEFUL SOLUTION

2144

AIR BASE

2145

AIRCRAFT CARRIER

2146

SUBMARINE

2147

PRODUCTION OF NUCLEAR WEAPONS

2148

PRODUCTION OF C WEAPONS

2149

SEA-DUMPED CHEMICAL WEAPONS

2150

RESEARCH IN DEFENSE AGAINST BIO WEAPONS

2151

... BELONGS TO THE DEFENSE MINISTRY

2152

... RECEIVES FUNDING

2153

... IN CO-OPERATION

2154

VEHICLES

2155

ARMS

2156

SHIPS

2157

ROCKETS

2158

ELECTRONICS

2159

ARTILLERY

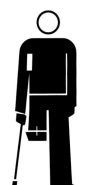

2160

SOLDIERS

2161

VICTIMS OF LANDMINES

2162

REFUGEES

2163

EXPORT OF SMALL ARMS

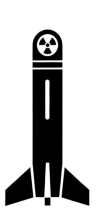

2164

NUCLEAR WARHEADS

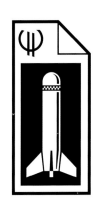

2165

DEFENSE BUDGET

LINGUA UNIVERSALIS

2166
FISH STOCK

2167
DAMAGE TO FISH STOCK

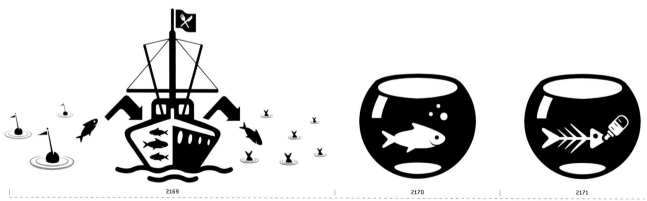

2169

2170

2171

2172

2173	2174	2175	2176	2177	2178
HERRING	MACKEREL	HAKE	ROSEFISH	SOLE	PLAICE

2179	2180	2181	2182	2183	2184
COD	COALFISH	HADDOCK	WHITING	HORSE MACKEREL	ANCHOVY

2185	2186	2187	2188	2189	2190
LING	ANGLER-FISH	POLLACK	SAND EEL	SPRAT	SMELT

2191	2192	2193	2194	2195	2196
INSIGNIFICANTLY EXPLOITED	MODERATELY EXPLOITED	EXPLOITED TO THE MAXIMUM	OVERFISHED	EXHAUSTED	UNDER RECONSTRUCTION

GREENPEACE MAGAZIN, 3/00: FARMERS AND SEED CORPORATIONS

LINGUA UNIVERSALIS

2198

BUY ECONOMICAL APPLIANCES

2199

SWITCH OFF FRIDGE WHILE ON VACATION

2200

CLEAN OVEN WINDOW

2201

BOIL WITH LITTLE WATER / USE GAS / USE AFTERGLOW OF HOTPLATES /PUT LID ON POT

2202

PUT FRIDGE IN COOL PLACE

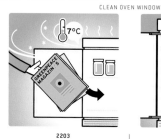

2203

FILL A CAVITY

2204

REGULAR DEFROSTING

2205

LET FRESH AIR IN FOR A SHORT TIME

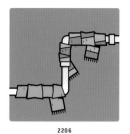

2206

INSULATE HEATING PIPES

2207

CHECK HEATING SYSTEM

2208

TURN DOWN THE HEATING

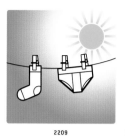

2209

WIND AND SUN TO DRY THE LAUNDRY

2210

USE ENERGY SAVING LAMP

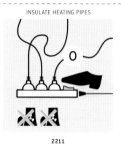

2211

PULL PLUG

2212

USE POWER-SAFER

2216

FORGET PRE-WASH AND BOILING WASH / ALWAYS FULLY LOAD TUB

2213

LIGHT BULBS IN BATHROOM

2214

SWITCH OFF COMPUTER

2215

TAKE A QUICK SHOWER

2217
POWER STATION ON ROOF / IN BASEMENT

2218
HEAT INSULATION OF EXTERNAL WALLS

2219
MICROWAVE ONLY IN SMALL AMOUNTS

2220
TOASTED BUNS

2221
BUY APPLIANCES WITHOUT BATTERIES

2222
SWITCH OFF LIGHTS

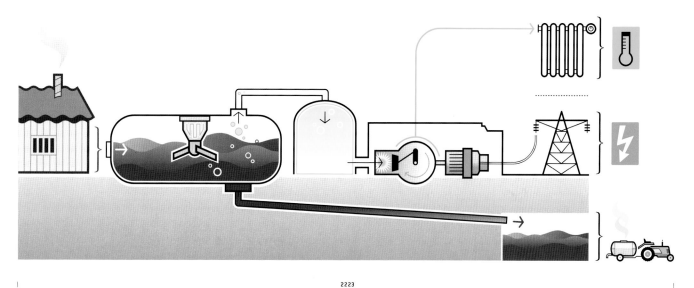

GPM, 6/03: REGENERATIVE ENERGY – BIOGAS PLANTS

2224 > 2261
GPM, 3/01: AGRICULTURAL MADNESS

| 2224 | 2225 | 2226 | 2227 |

| 2228 | 2229 | 2230 | 2231 | 2232 |

| 2233 | 2234 | 2235 | 2236 | 2237 |

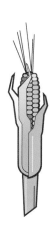

2238

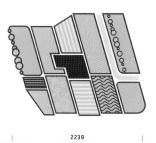

2239

2240

2241

2242

2243

2244

2245

2246

2247

SHIT

LINGUA UNIVERSALIS

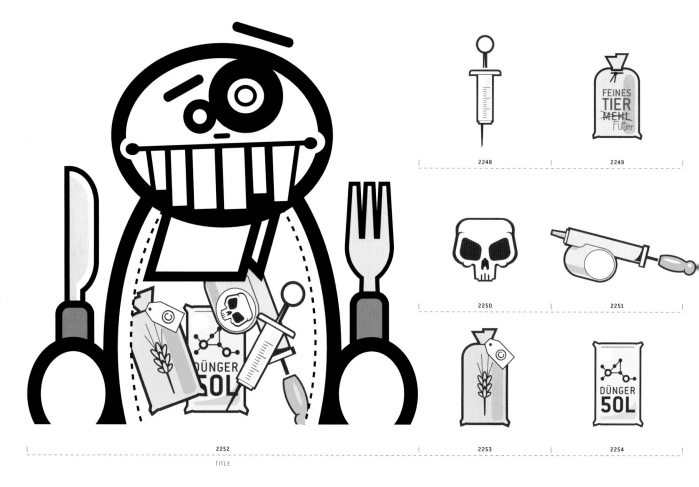

2248

2249

2250

2251

2253

2254

2255

CONSUMER

2256

EU-BUREAUCRAT

2257

CHICKEN-SEXER

2258

FARMER

2259

AGRO-INDUSTRIAL MANAGER

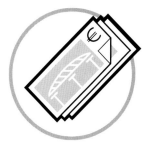

2260

EU-MONEY

2262

GPM, 1/02: ENVIRONMENTALLY FRIENDLY THINKING WITHOUT ACTION

LINGUA UNIVERSALIS

2263 > 2316
GPM, 5/02: NUCLEAR POWER - - - - - ->

| 2263 | 2264 | 2265 | 2266 |

| 2267 | 2268 | 2269 | 2270 | 2271 |

| 2272 | 2273 | 2274 | 2275 | 2276 |

2277

2278

2279

2280

2281

2282

2283

2284

2285

2286

2287

ATOMKRAFT? NEIN DANKE

www.greenpeace-magazin.de

2288

FINAL STICKER

LINGUA UNIVERSALIS

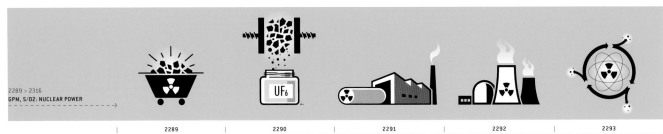

2289	2290	2291	2292	2293
URANIUM MINING	ENRICHMENT	PRODUCTION OF FUEL RODS	NUCLEAR POWER PRODUCTION	REPROCESSING OF NUCLEAR WASTE

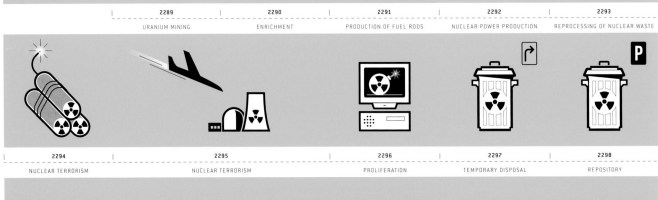

2294	2295	2296	2297	2298
NUCLEAR TERRORISM	NUCLEAR TERRORISM	PROLIFERATION	TEMPORARY DISPOSAL	REPOSITORY

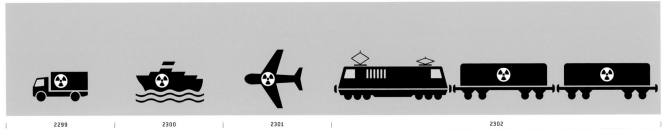

2299	2300	2301	2302
TRANSPORT BY LAND ...	... BY SEA ...	... BY AIR.	NUCLEAR WASTE TRANSPORT

2303

SMUGGLING / THEFT

2304 > 2308
GPM, 5/02: NUCLEAR POWER STATION ...

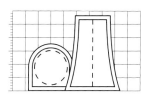

2304

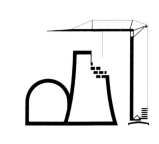

2305

... UNDER CONSTRUCTION

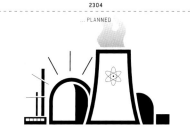

... PLANNED

2306

... IN OPERATION

2307

... CLOSED

2308

... RAMSHACKLE

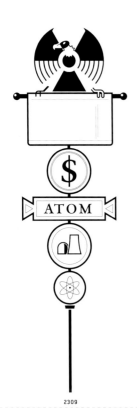

2309

2310

2311

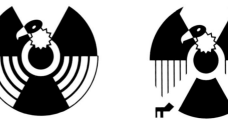

2312

2313

2314

2315

2316

NUCLEAR POWER RULES THE WORLD

2317

2318

2319

2320

2321

2322

2323

2324 > 2335
GREENPEACE MAGAZIN, 4/03: WOOD + PAPER
- ->

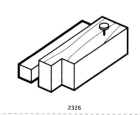

2324	2325	2326
WOOD (MATERIAL)	FURNITURE	CONSTRUCTION WOOD

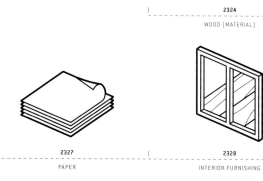

2327	2328	2329	2330
PAPER	INTERIOR FURNISHING	MUSICAL INSTRUMENTS	TOOL HANDLES

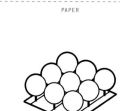

2331	2332	2333	2334
PLANTATION	TIMBER PLANTATION	PRIMEVAL FOREST	ECOLOGICAL FORESTRY

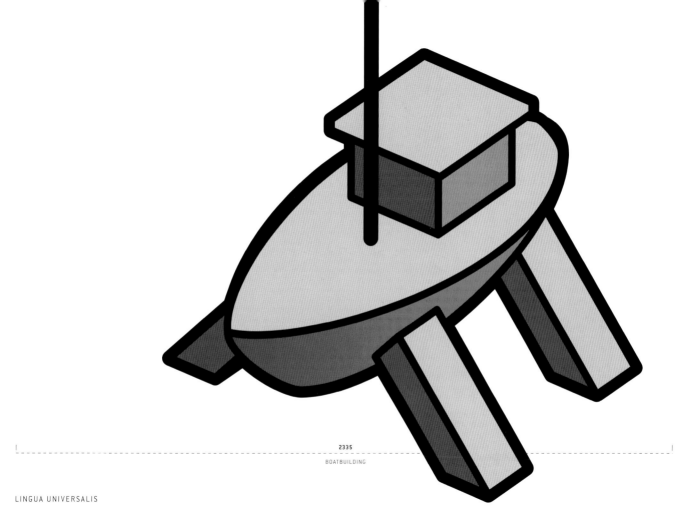

2335

BOATBUILDING

2336 > 2338
GREENPEACE MAGAZIN, 3/02: VARIOUS ILLUSTRATIONS

2336

NUCLEAR SPACE TRAVEL

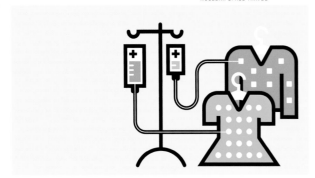

2337

PHARMACEUTICAL ACTIVE INGREDIENTS IN CLOTHING

2338

BACTERIA EATING POISON

2339 > 2523 L'OREAL

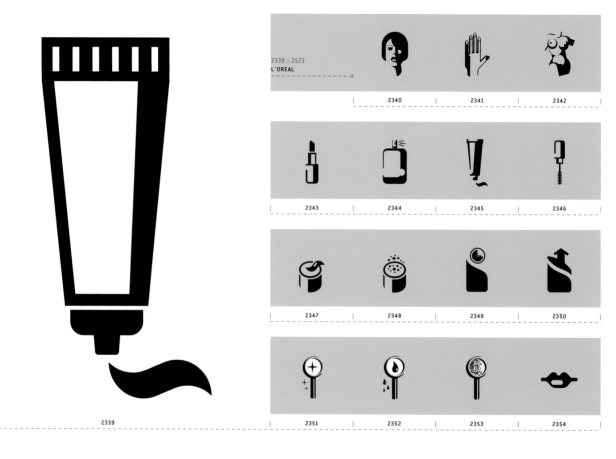

2339 > 2523

L'OREAL →

2339

| 2340 | 2341 | 2342 |

| 2343 | 2344 | 2345 | 2346 |

| 2347 | 2348 | 2349 | 2350 |

| 2351 | 2352 | 2353 | 2354 |

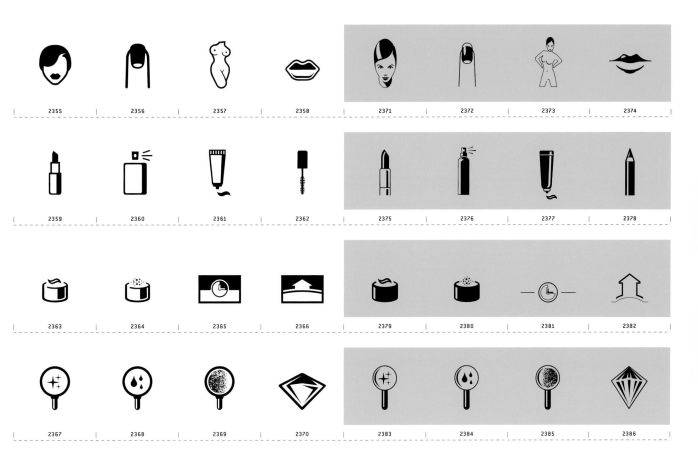

2355 | 2356 | 2357 | 2358 | 2371 | 2372 | 2373 | 2374

2359 | 2360 | 2361 | 2362 | 2375 | 2376 | 2377 | 2378

2363 | 2364 | 2365 | 2366 | 2379 | 2380 | 2381 | 2382

2367 | 2368 | 2369 | 2370 | 2383 | 2384 | 2385 | 2386

2387

2388

2389

2390

2393

2394

2395

2396

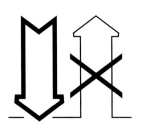

2391

2392

2397

2398

2399

2400

2403

2404

2405

2406

2401

2402

2407 2408

2409 2410

2411 2412

2413 2414

2415

2416

2417

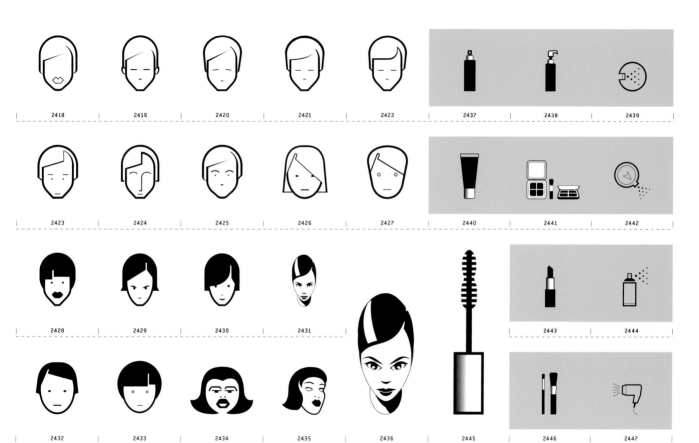

2418   2419   2420   2421   2422   2437   2438   2439

2423   2424   2425   2426   2427   2440   2441   2442

2428   2429   2430   2431   2443   2444

2432   2433   2434   2435   2436   2445   2446   2447

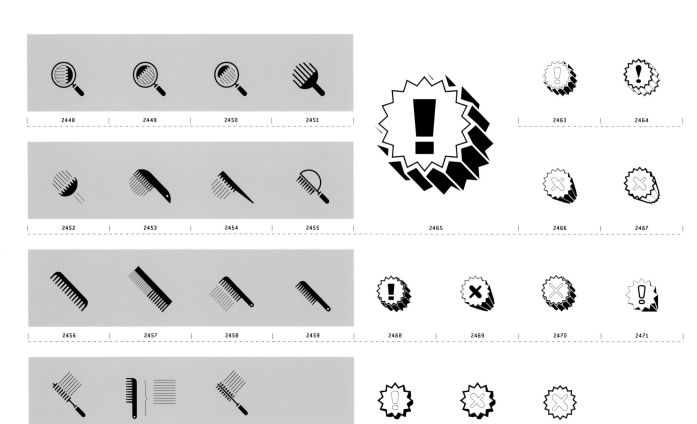

2448 2449 2450 2451

2452 2453 2454 2455

2456 2457 2458 2459

2460 2461 2462

2463 2464

2465

2466 2467

2468 2469 2470 2471

2472 2473 2474

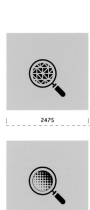

2475

2479

2480

2487

2488

2494

2476

2481

2482

2489

2490

2495

2498

2477

2483

2484

2491

2492

2496

2478

2485

2486

2493

24997

2499

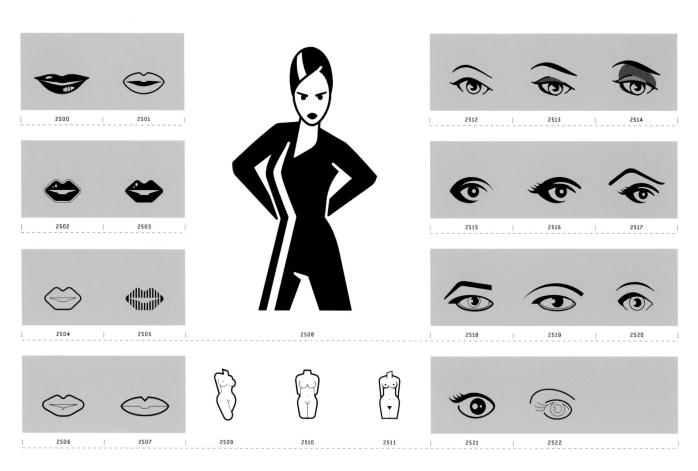

2500 2501

2502 2503

2504 2505

2506 2507

2508

2509 2510 2511

2512 2513 2514

2515 2516 2517

2518 2519 2520

2521 2522

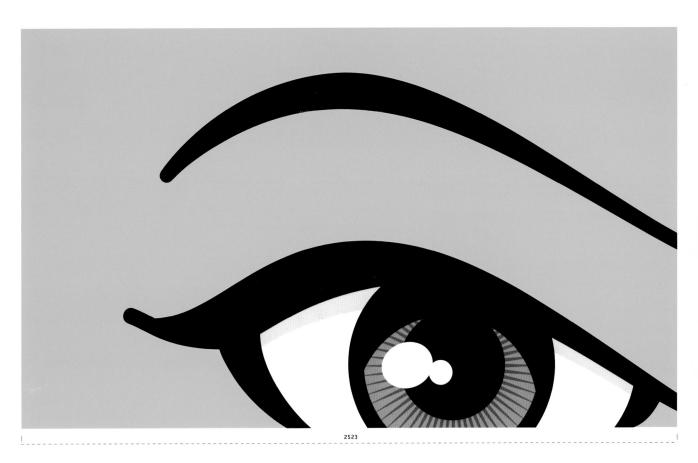

2523

2524 > 2568
MX, GRAND MAGASIN

2524	2525	2526	2527
COME IN...	... FIND OUT	LIFT	RESTAURANT

2528	2529	2530	2531	2532	2533
DOGGY LOO	GENTLEMEN	LADIES	WHEELCHAIR	BABY-CARE	HELIPORT

2535	2536	2537	2538	2539	2540
STAY ...	... AMUSED ...	... CONSUME!	STAY ...	... AMUSED ...	... CONSUME!

2534	2541	2542	2543	2544	2545	2546
BUGGY SERVICE	STAY ...	... AMUSED ...	... CONSUME!	GRAND MAGASIN	GRAND MAGASIN	MUTABOR X

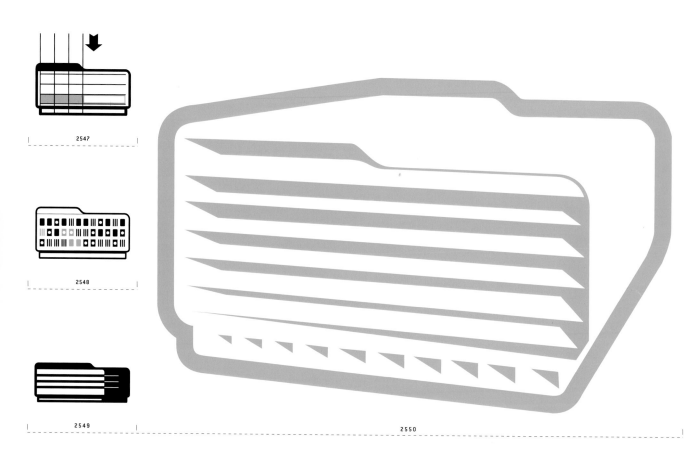

2547

2548

2549

2550

2551

INFORMATIONSGEFÜHL

2552

SENIOR

2553

MIDDLE-AGED

2554

JUNIOR

2555

SIBELLE

2556

PATRICE

2557

CHEESEBURGER ...

2558

... PLUS EXTRA ONIONS!

2559

2560

2561

2562

2563

SENIOR PRODUCT

2564

MIDDLE-AGED PRODUCT

2565

JUNIOR PRODUCT

2566

2567

2568

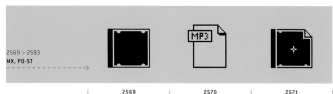

2569	2570	2571
MUSIC MEDIA	MUSIC DATA	DATA DELUXE

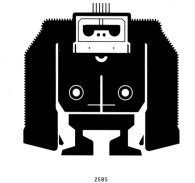

2572	2573	2574	2575
INFRA RED	RESIST!	ONE-PLUS-THREE	NANO CACHE

2584

2585

PAST

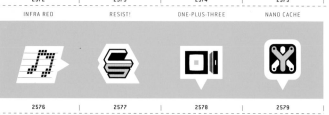

2576	2577	2578	2579
PIXELLENCE	CUBISTIC SOUND	N.O.I.S.E.	VINYLATOR

2580	2581	2582	2583
LOUD SPEAKER	POWER CELL	POST-CARD	LIFT

2586

2587

PRESENT

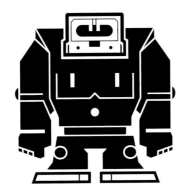

2597 > 2598

MX, FLAT WATCHES
- - - - - - - - - - - - - ->

2597

FLAT, LOGO

2588

2589

FUTURE

2590

PLANET OF THE TAPES

2591

DEMOTAPES, LOGO

2592

VINYL

2593

COMPACT DISK

2594 > 2596

MX, SUBZERO CLOTHING
- - - - ->

2594

MUTATION TECHNOLOGY

2595

GM MOTIONTRACKER

2596

MASTERCUT TECHNOLOGY

2598

FLAT WATCHFACE: AIRPORT

LINGUA UNIVERSALIS

2599 > 2616
MX, DENTAMATE ORAL HYGIENE
- - - - - - - - - - - - - - - - - >

2599

2600

2601

2602

2603

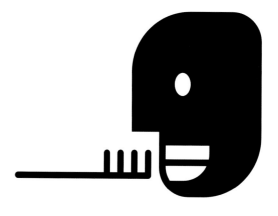

2607

2604

2605

2606

MAMAN, JE VEUX AVOIR ...

2608

MAXIMUM SAFETY

2609

FRESH TASTE

2610

GREAT LOOKS

2611

2612

DEEP SEA PREDATOR

2613

SQUEEEEEEZE!

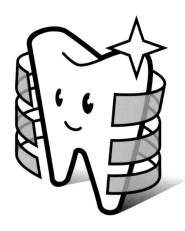

2614

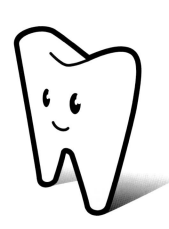

2615

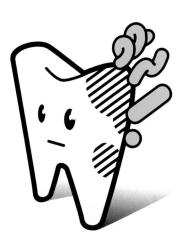

2616

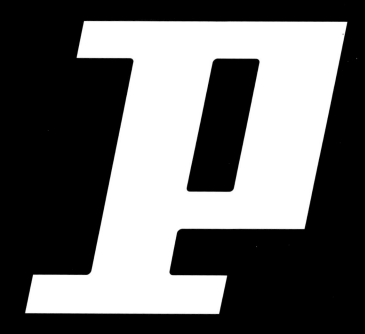

2617 > 2661 PREMIUM

MCF TURBO (MUTABOR CUSTOMIZED FONT)

2617

2618

2619

2620

2621

2622

2623

2624

2625

2626

2627	2628	2629	2630
SLOWER	FASTER	LOW ON AIR	OUT OF AIR

2631	2632	2633	2634
ME	YOU	STOP! ATTENTION	NO

2635	2636	2637	2637
THAT WAY	HELP! EMERGENCY	OPENING SPARES	REGROUP

2639

ENTOXICATED

2640

OK

2641

EARS NOT CLEARING

2642

DID NOT UNDERSTAND

2643

GOING DOWN

2644

GOING UP

2645

SOMETHING IS WRONG

LINGUA UNIVERSALIS

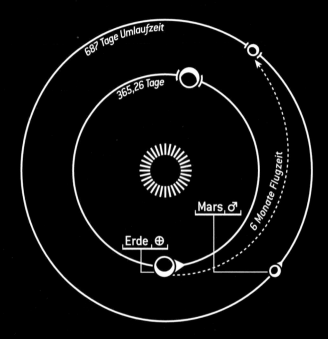

687 Tage Umlaufzeit

365,26 Tage

6 Monate Flugzeit

Mars ♂

Erde ⊕

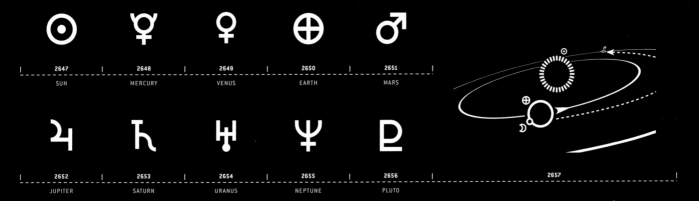

2647	2648	2649	2650	2651
SUN	MERCURY	VENUS	EARTH	MARS

2652	2653	2654	2655	2656	2657
JUPITER	SATURN	URANUS	NEPTUNE	PLUTO	

2658	2659	2660	2661
FIRST MAN ON MOON	SPACE STATION	FIRST WALK IN SPACE	FIRST MAN IN SPACE

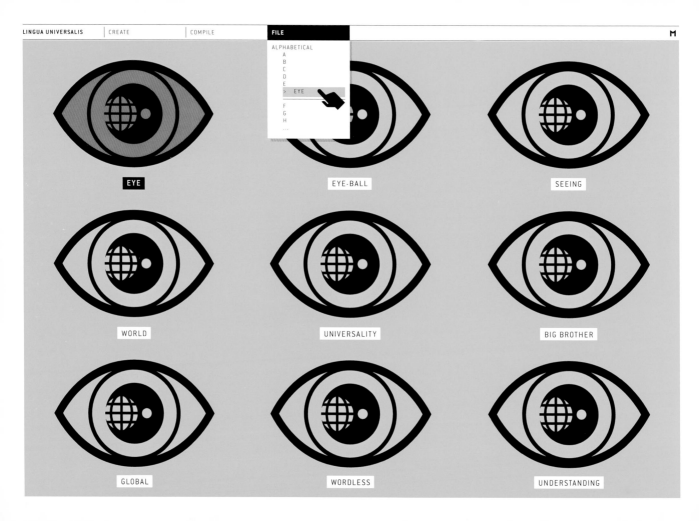

ILLEGAL STREET-ART, 1

29/06/03 10:36:49, AMSTERDAM, NL

ILLEGAL STREET-ART, 2

01/07/03 15:45:03, AMSTERDAM, NL

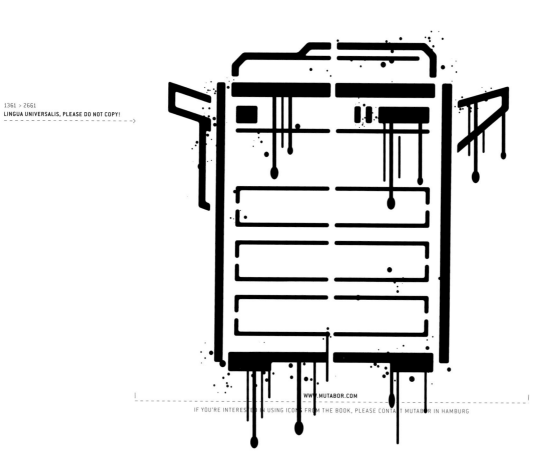

WWW.MUTABOR.COM